THE HISTORIE
OF THE LYFF OF
JAMES MELVILL

THE HISTORIE
OF THE LYFF OF
JAMES MELVILL

A SELECTION

EDITED BY
J. G. FYFE

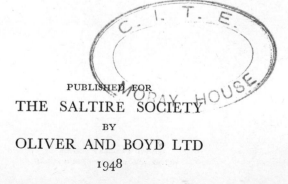

PUBLISHED FOR
THE SALTIRE SOCIETY
BY
OLIVER AND BOYD LTD
1948

First Edition .   .   .   1948

The Editor wishes to express his thanks to Professor J. D. Mackie who read the first draft of the preliminary matter, and to Mr James Fergusson who read the proofs and made some very helpful suggestions.

PRINTED IN GREAT BRITAIN BY
OLIVER AND BOYD LTD., EDINBURGH

INTRODUCTION

To the historian James Melville is invaluable. He wrote of what he saw, of what he experienced, of contemporary opinion as expressed to him by the men whom he met daily ; as a child he listened to the discussions between the Reformed ministers who gathered round his father's fireside, as a student he heard John Knox preach, and when he reached man's estate he became, partly by his own worth and partly through his association with his Uncle Andrew, a leading man in the Kirk. He knew what the King was thinking, for the King told him frequently, and in Presbytery and General Assembly he was made aware of what was in the minds not only of his fellow-ministers but also of the laity.

The conflict which Melville describes is one which has had many analogues (both political and religious) throughout the centuries, not least of all in the twentieth century. On the one side was the Reformed Kirk striving to establish itself, trying to win freedom to think and worship as it wanted, and at the same time trying to coerce others to its point of view ; on the other side was a self-opinionated monarch believing in Divine Right and in the necessity of a subordinate episcopacy to maintain in the Church that good order without which he considered a settled State could not be achieved. The King's despotic tendencies were fostered by a baronage eager to share in the patrimony of the pre-Reformation Church and by those at home and abroad who sought a restoration of Roman Catholicism. The Kirk, too, had a large and influential following amongst the peers and the lairds—how far it was championed by the commonalty (except in the towns) it is difficult to assess. Of this struggle with all its incidental complexities James Melville is the contemporary observer *par excellence*.

Melville, of course, was not impartial, and he knew exactly where he stood. " Sall the Kirk of Jesus Chryst," he wrote, " be les regardit and restranit in hir fredome privilage, in a setlit and constitut esteat, under the protectioun of a rare Christian Magistrat ? God forbid ! " But he was essentially a truthful man telling a " suthfast " story, and his narrative unconsciously reveals the weaknesses of the ministers and the errors and excesses into which their fervour led them.

The dominating figure in the book is James Melville's uncle, Andrew Melville. There never were two men who loved one another more, and James's story of how he first heard of Andrew, asked his father about him, was told that he had not been heard of for many years, and then discovered him for himself, is a piece of true literary art—all the more effective because it is artless. The popular conception of Andrew is indicated by his contemporary nickname of " The Blast "—a not unjust sobriquet for one who, like so many of his brethren, did injury to himself and to his cause by his zealous indiscretions of speech. James faithfully records the more glaring instances of Andrew's outspokenness, though affection and hero-worship do not allow him to see them as faults, but he also tells many other things of him ; " The Blast " is forgotten and in his place stands a very learned man with a ready wit, a keen sense of humour, a pleasure in common-room gossip, and great powers both as ecclesiastic and educationalist. Indeed, one of the strongest feelings aroused by James's " Lyff " is surprise at the scholarship and dateless humanity of Melville and his contemporaries. Another is a firm conviction of their passionate sincerity. Faults they had and to spare—they were, for example, relentless to the point of cruelty in their condemnation of immorality and of those who would usurp the prerogatives of " Chryst the King "—but these were the faults of the age. Take them away and there is left a very human, very likeable body of men, any one of whom would be a welcome friend today.

His nephew's hero-worship and the force of his own personality make Andrew dominate the book, but James still remains the hero. It is essentially his book—a personal record of a man cultured, kindly, mild in character, yet steadfast in his faith. In temperament he was the exact opposite of Andrew and for this reason was overshadowed when he engaged in matters which have now become history. But he never forgot that he was writing the story of his own life and there is a perennial interest in his full account of his childhood, of his education, of his student life at St Andrews, and of his domestic and other affairs in later life. He is charmingly naïve about it all, whether he is dealing with his conversion, or his sins, or his matrimonial arrangements, or his adventures in sea-sickness. Altogether a " maist lovabill " man and a " maist lovabill " book.

The title which Melville inscribed on his manuscript is " The Historie of the Lyff of James Melvill " but the book is generally known as *The Autobiography and Diary of Mr James Melville*. The only contemporary manuscript is in the National Library of Scotland, and is probably the original since it contains many additional passages and marginal notes which have obviously been added at various times, but which are all in the same hand as the manuscript itself. This manuscript was at one time in the possession of David Calderwood who made great use of it in his *History of the Kirk of Scotland*—indeed, most historians who have written of Scotland in the latter half of the sixteenth century have drawn largely from James Melville, and there seem to have been several transcripts in existence in the seventeenth and eighteenth centuries. " The Historie of the Lyff of James Melvill " was first printed by the Bannatyne Club in 1829 (with the title *The Diary of Mr James Melvill*),

and in 1842 the Wodrow Society issued an edition (with
the title *The Autobiography and Diary of Mr James Melville*)
edited by Robert Pitcairn. The text of the latter has
been used in this selection. Pitcairn also included in
his volume " A True Narratioune of the Declyneing Aige
of the Kirk of Scotland from MDXCVI to MDCX,"
to which he gave the sub-title " Being a Continuation
of Mr James Melvill's Diary." No passages from this
continuation have been used here, mainly because the
task of selection from the 500 pages of the " Lyff " was
formidable enough without the addition of another 300
pages. So far as space permitted, an attempt has been
made to give a satisfactory picture of James Melville by
himself and of Andrew Melville by his nephew, to give a
fairly detailed view of university life in the sixteenth
century, and to give some idea of the points at issue
in the struggle between Kirk and King and of how both
sides conducted their campaigns. No effort has been
made to achieve continuity (an impossibility in such a
short book) but explanatory footnotes have been added
where necessary and there is a brief biographical note
on every person mentioned. Considerations of space
have precluded documentation.

At first Melville's language may seem to the modern
reader to be rather formidable, but it is not really so.
True, he uses many words that are unfortunately no
longer current, and his spelling is highly individual and
refreshingly inconsistent, but the main difficulties are
dealt with in glossarial footnotes, and words which are
not glossed will generally reveal their secret if they are
pronounced phonetically.

SHORT BIBLIOGRAPHY

CALDERWOOD, DAVID. *The History of the Kirk of Scotland* (Wodrow
    Society, 1842-1845).
FLEMING, D. HAY. *The Reformation in Scotland* (London, 1910).
M'CRIE, THOMAS. *Life of Andrew Melville* (Edinburgh, 1855).
MOYSIE, DAVID. *Memoirs of the Affairs of Scotland, 1577-1603* (Banna-
    tyne Club, 1830).

Row, John. *The History of the Kirk of Scotland, 1558-1637* (Wodrow Society, 1842).

Spottiswoode, John. *History of the Church of Scotland, 203-1625* (Edinburgh, 1851).

Thomson, Thomas (editor). *The Booke of the Universall Kirk of Scotland* (Bannatyne Club, 1839-1845).

BIOGRAPHICAL NOTES

James Melville (1556-1614), son of Richard Melville of Baldovy, minister of Marytoun near Montrose, and of Isabel Scrymgeour ; student at St Andrews University, 1569-1573 ; regent at Glasgow University, 1575-1580 ; Professor of Hebrew and Oriental Languages at St Andrews University, 1580 ; strong supporter of his uncle's Presbyterian views ; fled to Berwick in 1584 owing to threat of reprisals for his persistent exposure of Archbishop Adamson's malpractices ; went to Newcastle and London and returned to Scotland in November 1585 ; called to parish of Anstruther-Wester with which were combined the parishes of Pittenweem, Abercrombie, and Kilrenny, 1586 ; by 1590 had resigned all parishes except Kilrenny, to which charge he then devoted himself ; continued teaching at St Andrews ; summoned to London by James VI and I, 1606 ; sent into ward at Newcastle, 1607 ; died at Berwick when on way back to Scotland ; married (1) 1583, Elizabeth (d. 1609), daughter of John Durie, minister of Edinburgh. (2) 1612, Debora, daughter of Richard Clerke, vicar of Berwick-on-Tweed.

Andrew Melville (1545-1622), youngest son of Richard Melville of Baldovy (James Melville's grandfather) and of Giles Abercrombie ; his father fell at Pinkie, 1547, and his mother died soon after ; he was brought up by his eldest brother and his wife (James Melville's parents) ; student at St Andrews, 1559 ; went to Paris to complete education, 1564 ; went to Poitiers, 1566, and appointed regent in University ; helped to defend town during siege, 1568 ; when siege raised, went to Geneva and, through influence of Beza, appointed Professor of Humanity ; returned to Scotland, 1574 ; Principal of Glasgow University, 1574 ; revised, extended, and modernised the curriculum, and, later, helped to reform the Universities of Aberdeen and St Andrews ; his unceasing efforts to secure the establishment of Presbyterianism in Scotland brought him into frequent conflict with James VI ; Principal of St Mary's College, St Andrews, 1580 ; charged with treason, 1584 ; fled to England, but returned to Scotland in 1585 after fall of Arran ; Rector of St Andrews University, 1590-1599 ; defied the King and was summoned to London, 1606 ; wrote epigram against ritual of Anglican Church and was sent to the Tower, 1607 ; released in 1611 on petition of the Duke of Bouillon and was appointed Professor of Biblical Theology at the University of Sedan, a post which he held till his death ; Melville was a brilliant scholar, a great educationalist, and a very able administrator, but in ecclesiastical affairs the intemperance of his language and his uncompromising attitude hindered the cause which he so zealously upheld.

TABLE OF EVENTS

This table is not, and is not intended to be, a complete summary of the period 1560-1601—its purpose is to indicate broadly what happened, and to show in their proper setting the events mentioned in the text.

1560 (August).—Estates ratified the Confession of Faith (" The Scots Confession "), thus giving parliamentary approval to the Reformed Faith. But legal establishment of the Reformed Church was refused, mainly because the Reformers claimed the Teinds and the whole revenue and possessions of the Roman Catholic Church. The Estates also annulled the authority of the Pope and made celebration of or attendance at Mass penal offences.

1560 (December).—First General Assembly met. There is no record that either it or any subsequent Assembly gave formal approval to either *The Book of Common Order* (Knox's Liturgy) or *The First Book of Discipline*—they were probably regarded as accepted standards, and this is certainly the implication of the first reference to *The Book of Common Order* in *The Booke of the Universall Kirk* (December 1562). It is known that *The Book of Common Order* had been adopted by some congregations prior to December 1560. *The First Book of Discipline* was completed in May 1560 and first mentioned in *The Booke of the Universall Kirk* a year later. The Estates discussed it in January 1561 but refused to sanction it.

1561.—Privy Council allocated part of one-third of the benefices of the pre-Reformation Church to provide stipends for the Reformed clergy. The other part of one-third was retained by the Crown, but as both parts were collected by the Crown in the first instance, very little of the money reached the Church and few stipends were paid till 1567 when the arrangement was embodied in an Act of Parliament (see p. 17). The remaining two-thirds of the benefices were retained by the actual holders (lay and clerical) of benefices.

1567.—James VI succeeded. Moray regent (p. 22).

1570.—Moray assassinated. Lennox regent.

1571.—Lennox shot. Mar regent.

1572.—Mar died. Morton regent. Death of John Knox. In January 1572 a Convention of the Kirk at Leith reached an agreement between Kirk and State for the retention of the old dioceses and the appointment by the State of bishops who should be subject in spiritual matters to the General Assembly. This was confirmed by the General Assembly in August, but the Assembly also approved a unanimous protest that the arrangement was not ideal and that they regarded it as only temporary. In point of fact, this introduction of pseudo-bishops, who were nicknamed " Tulchans " (see p. 31), was an astute move by Morton to secure for himself and other leaders of the King's party the two-thirds of the revenue of the pre-Reformation dioceses which had been retained by the actual holders in 1560. The holders of these benefices were now dying out and Morton aimed at appointing one of his own creatures to a vacant see, paying him a pittance, and appropriating the rest of the revenue.

1575.—Andrew Melville returned from Geneva, a convinced Calvinist, and began to agitate for the abolition of episcopacy as " unscriptural."

1578.—Morton resigned regency. James VI's personal rule began.

1580.—General Assembly declared Episcopacy unlawful and ordered bishops to resign.

1581.—General Assembly resolved that " the Booke of Policie aggreit to befor, in diverse Assemblies, sould be registrat in the Acts of the Kirk." This was the book now known as *The Second Book of Discipline* which had been completed about five years before, approved by various Assemblies, and discussed by representatives of the Church and of the Privy Council in an unsuccessful effort to have it accepted by the State (see under 1592).

James VI subscribed the King's Confession (" Negative Confession ")—a denunciation of Roman Catholicism which was intended to reassure the suspicious and strongly Calvinistic Kirk. Effect nullified by King's own actions and by growing evidence that he was developing his theory of Divine Right. Kirk and State now in open conflict.

1582.—Kirk seething with rumours of " Popish " plots in which courtiers, and perhaps even the King, were said to be involved. John Durie (see p. 43) was expelled from Edinburgh after an outspoken sermon against the King. In August the Ruthven Raid took place—certain nobles seized the King's person, and the Kirk approved, claiming that the Raid had caused the failure of the plots. The King escaped and was furious with the Kirk, which refused to retract.

1584.—Andrew Melville summoned before Council to answer for his utterances (p. 50) and claimed that only the Presbytery could initiate proceedings against him. He was condemned by Council and fled to Berwick.

King secured the passage by Parliament of the Black Acts, five in all, the cumulative effect of which was to suppress Presbytery and the liberty of the Church and, by strengthening the power of the bishops, to subject the Church to the royal will even in spiritual matters.

1585.—Arran, King's favourite and Kirk's evil genius, fell from power.

1586.—Arran banished. Ministers and Church courts regained much of their freedom through compromise—bishops remained but were now answerable for their conduct to the General Assembly and were to work in conjunction with the Church courts.

1587.—James reached his majority. He secured passage of an Act for the "Annexation of the Temporalitie of benefices to the Crown." The "spirituality" (i.e. the teinds) remained as before, two-thirds attached to bishoprics, the remaining third divided between Crown and Kirk. The Kirk accepted this Act, thinking that the loss of temporalities would weaken the chances of a restoration of a true episcopacy.

1588.—Spanish Armada (see p. 54).

1592.—Since 1585 relations between King and Kirk had been steadily improving, and in 1592 the Kirk achieved all its aims with the passage of the Golden Act ("Ratification of the liberty of the trew Kirk : of Generall and Synodal assemblie : of Presbyteries : of discipline," etc.). This Act established the Kirk on a Presbyterian basis and gave legal authority to the main principles of "The Book of Policy" (*Second Book of Discipline*), though the Book itself was not mentioned. This Act was largely the work of Chancellor Thirlstane.

1595.—Thirlstane died and the King, left to his own devices, began to reassert his Divine Right. Even as early as 1593, however, relations between him and the Kirk had been strained because of leniency to Roman Catholic nobles who were plotting with Spain (pp. 59-66). After Thirlstane's death the position deteriorated and extravagant sermons against the King were preached by many of the ministers.

1596 (October).—David Black, minister of St Andrews, preached a sermon in which he called Queen Elizabeth an atheist and made a bitter attack on James and his Court ("Are not all kings devil's bairns ?"). The English Ambassador complained to the King and Black was summoned before the Privy Council but declined its judicature. Undignified bickering ensued, the Kirk lost the sympathies of many moderate men, and the King determined that episcopacy must be re-established in order to curb the ministers and control the Kirk (see p. 62).

1597.—King summoned an extraordinary General Assembly to meet at Perth, hoping that more ministers from north of the Tay would attend and fewer from the unruly districts of Fife and the

Lothians. The ministers of the north were out of sympathy with the ultra-Presbyterianism of Fife and the Lothians, and James hoped that this Assembly at Perth would be more amenable to his wishes. It was. James was delighted and summoned another Assembly at Dundee in May. The ministers of the north again came in force and James secured the appointment of a permanent commission of fourteen leading ministers who, though given wide powers, were under his domination.

1598.—At a General Assembly which he summoned to Dundee (and from which he excluded Andrew Melville), the King gained approval for a scheme, which he had already discussed with the Commission, that the clergy should be represented in Parliament.

1600.—General Assembly met at Montrose in March and agreed that it should submit names of possible Parliamentary Commissioners to the King who should make the final choice. In August the King was involved in the Gowrie Conspiracy, as a result of which he again came to loggerheads with the extremists in the Kirk (p. 74).

1602.—General Assembly decided that ministers should be appointed to all vacant sees. This, together with the decisions of 1598 and 1600 regarding members of the Assembly sitting in Parliament as a spiritual estate, was in everything but name a reintroduction of episcopacy.

I knawe a man in Chryst, brought from the wombe of his mother be God, the 25 day of the monethe July, (dedicat of auld to S. James the Apostle and Martyr,) in the yeir of our Lord 1556 [1]; wha, for thankfulness of hart, to the praise and honour of his gratius God and deir father in Chryst, and for edification and comfort of his childring, and sic as sall reid the saming heirefter, is movit to sett down, in monument of wryt, the benefets of God bestowit on him sen his first conception and day of his birthe foremarked ; sa far, at leist, as his weak understanding and freall memorie in maters that ar esteimed of importancc can conceave and recompt. Whowbeit, as I haiff professed, in the words of the Psalme with David, that the smalest of his unknawin benefits passes the graittest reatche of my apprehension and utterance.

[1] " My uncle, Mr Andro, haulds that I was born *in anno* 1557." Margin of MS.

THE HISTORIE OF THE LYFF OF
JAMES MELVILL

HIS MOTHER AND HIS UNCLE ANDREW

I haiff often hard Mr Andro [1] say, that he being a
bern verie seiklie, was maist lovinglie and tenderlie
treated and cared for be hir, embrasing him and kissing
him oftentymes, with these words, " God giff me an uther
lad lyk thie, and syne tak me to his rest ! "   Now sche haid
haid twa laddies befor me, wharof the eldest was dead ;
and betwix him and the second, sche bure thrie lasses ;
sa, in end, God granted hir desyre, and gaiff hir an,
wha wald to God he war als lyk to Mr Andro in gifts
of mynd as he is thought to be in proportion of bodie
and lineaments of face ; for ther is nane, that is nocht
utherwayes particularlie informed, bot taks me for Mr
Andro's brother.

MEMORIES OF CHILDHOOD : EARLY EDUCATION

I haid an evill-inclyned woman to my nuris [2] ;
therefter speaned [3] and put in a cottar hous, and about
four or fyve yeir auld brought hame to a step-mother ;
yit a verie honest burges of Montros [Robert Clark] [4]
hes oft tauld me, that my father wald ley me down on my
bak, pleying with mie, and lauche at me because I could
nocht ryse, I was sa fatt ; and wald ask mie what ealed
mie : I wald answer, " I am sa fatt I may nocht geang."
And trewlie sen my rememberance, I cam never to the
place bot God moved sum an with a motherlie affection

---

[1] Andrew Melville (see p. 9).
[2] His mother died within a year of his birth.
[3] weaned.
[4] Throughout this book, words written by Melville in the margins of
his MS. are printed in square brackets.

towardis me. About the fyft yeir of my age, the Grate Buik was put in my hand, and when I was seavine, lytle thairof haid I lernit at hame ; therfor my father put my eldest and onlie brother, David, about a year and a halff in age above me, and me togidder, to a kinsman and brother in the ministerie of his, to scholl, a guid, lerned, kynd man ; whome for thankfulnes I name, Mr Wilyam Gray, minister at Logie-Montrose.[1] He haid a sistar, a godlie and honest matron, rewlar of his hous, wha often rememberit me of my mother, and was a verie loving mother to us, indeid. Ther was a guid nomber of gentle and honest men's berns of the cowntrey about, weill treaned upe bathe in letters, godlines, and exerceise of honest geames. Ther we lerned to reid the Catechisme, Prayers, and Scripture ; to rehers the Catechisme and Prayers *par ceur* ; also nottes of Scripture, efter the reiding thairof ; and ther first I fand, (blysed be my guid God for it !) that Sprit of sanctification beginning to work sum motiones in my hart, even about the aught and nynt yeir of my age ; to pray going to bed and rysing, and being in the fields alan to say ower the prayers I haid lernit with a sweit moving in my hart ; and to abhore swearing, and rebuk and complean upon sic as I hard swear. Wherunto the exemple of that godlie matron, seiklie, and giffen to read and pray in hir bed, did mikle profit me ; for I ley in hir chamber and heard hir exerceises. We lerned ther the Rudiments of the Latin Grammair, withe the vocables in Latin and Frenche ; also dyverse speitches in Frenche, with the reiding and right pronunciation of that toung. We proceidit fordar to the Etymologie of Lilius and his Syntax, as also a lytle of the Syntax of Linacer ; therwith was joyned Hunter's Nomenclatura, the Minora Colloquia of Erasmus, and sum of the Eclogs of Virgill and Epistles of Horace ; also Cicero his Epistles *ad Terentiam*. He haid a verie guid and profitable form of resolving the authors ; he teatched grammaticallie, bathe according

[1] Was minister of Logie-Montrose in 1563. He died in 1602 or 1603.

to the Etymologie and Syntax ; bot as for me, the
trewthe was, my ingyne [1] and memorie war guid aneuche,
bot my judgment and understanding war as yit smored [2]
and dark, sa that the thing quhilk I gat was mair be rat
ryme [3] nor knawlage. Ther also we haid the aire guid,
and fields reasonable fear, and be our maister war
teached to handle the bow for archerie, the glub for goff,
the batons for fencing, also to rin, to loope, to swoom, to
warsell, to preve pratteiks,[4] everie ane haiffing his matche
and andagonist, bathe in our lessons and play. A happie
and golden tyme, indeid, giff our negligence and unthank-
fullnes haid nocht moved God to schorten it, partlie be
deceying [5] of the number, quhilk caused the maister to
weirie, and partlie be a pest quhilk the Lord, for sinne
and contempt of his Gospell, send upon Montrose,
distant from Over Logie bot twa myles ; sa that scholl
skalled,[6] and we war all send for and brought hame.
I was at that scholl the space of almost fyve yeirs, in the
quhilk tyme, of publict news I remember I hard of
[the mariage of Hendrie and Marie, King and Quein of
Scots,] Seingnour Davie's slauchter, of the King's
mourder at the Kirk of Field, of the Quein's taking at
Carbarri, and the Langsyd feild. Whereof reid Mr
Bowchannan Cornicle, lib. 17, 18, 19.
    Even at that tyme, me thought the heiring of these
things moved me, and stak in my hart with sum joy or
sorrow, as I hard they might helpe or hender the
Relligion : Namelie, I remember the ordour of the fast
keipit *in anno* 1566 ; the evill handling of the ministerie
be taking away of their stipends [7] ; for Mr James Melvill,

---

[1] mind (ingenuity).   [2] smothered, hidden.   [3] by rote.
[4] to learn by experience.   [5] decaying.   [6] was dispersed or dismissed.
[7] After the Reformation the teinds (or tithes) of the pre-Reformation
Church fell into the hands of the Crown and of various laymen, and the
ministers of the Reformed Church were " defrauded of their stipendis,
swa that they ar becummin in great povertie and necessity." After a
bitter struggle an Act of 1567 assigned part of one-third of the teinds
to the Reformed Church (see p. 10). Even this inadequate grant was
withheld and for several years many of the ministers were paid no stipends
at all.

B

my uncle,[1] and Mr James Balfour,[2] his cusing-german, bathe ministers and stipendles, with guid, godlie, and kynd Patrick Forbes of Cors.[3] The Lard of Kinnaber,[4] and the godlie and zealus gentlemen of the countrey, partlie for thair bernes' cause, and partlie for that notable instrument in the Kirk of Scotland, Jhone Erskine of Done,[5] Superintendent of Merns and Angus, his residence in Logy at certean tymes, did oftentymes frequent our hous, and talk of sic maters. Also, I remember weill whow we past to the head of the muir to sie the fyre of joy [6] burning upon the stiple head of Montrose, [at the day of the King's birthe.] These things I mark for the grait benefit of that place and companie, wherin the Lord wald haiff me treaned upe in my first and tender age.

Now, when my brother and I war come hame, our father examined us, and was glad to sie that we had profited reasonablie : Nevertheless, the esteat of the countrey was sa uncertain and troublesome, the moyen [7] he haid (wanting his awin stipend, and helping diverse that wanted of his breithring) bot mean and small, and the occasione of scholles nocht serving, we remeaned a wintar at hame, rememberit of our buiks bot now and then, as our father haid leaser, quhilk was bot verie seindle.[8] Yit the Lord sufferit nocht that tyme to be fruittles nather, bot I remember therin twa benefites ;

---

[1] James Melville (d. 1596), after holding various charges, became minister of Arbroath in 1580. He was Andrew Melville's brother. In 1566 he was minister of Fearn.

[2] James Balfour (d. 1613) held various charges before becoming minister of St Giles (2nd charge) in 1598. In 1566 he was minister of Idvie. He married Andrew Melville's sister Barbara.

[3] Patrick Forbes of Corse in Aberdeenshire, the father of Patrick Forbes who became Bishop of Aberdeen in 1618. The Forbeses were related to the Melvilles.

[4] John Fullarton of Kynnaber in Forfar, one of those who, in 1569, were "thoght apt and able be the ministers and commissionars forsaids to minister." (Booke of the Universall Kirk, i, 4.)

[5] Sir John Erskine of Dun (1509-1591), a leading Reformer.

[6] bonfire—James VI's birthday was 19th June.

[7] means of subsistence.   [8] seldom.

ane the reiding of the Storie of the Scripture that wintar, quhilk stak in my mynd ; and of David Lindsayes book,[1] quhilk my eldest sistare, Isbel, wald reid and sing, namlie, concerning the letter judgment, the peanes of hell, and the joyes of heavin, wherby scho wald caus me bathe greit and be glad. I lovit hir, therfor, exceiding deirlie, and scho me by [2] the rest.

THE SCHOOL AT MONTROSE IN 1569

About the spring tyme, my father resolved to keipe my eldar brother at hame withe him, to lern him housbandrie and experience of the warldlie lyff, now almost past from the age of bernheid ; and to send me to the scholl againe for a yeir or twa, that therefter he might acquent me also with housbandrie, and prepear for me a roum [3] ; and that becaus he nather saw the meanes to mak us attein to sic lerning as we might live upon, nor when we haid gottin it, anie sure interteinment in the countrey for it. Sa I was put to the scholl of Montrose ; finding, of God's guid providence, my auld mother, Marjorie Gray,[4] wha parting from hir brother at his mariage, haid taken upe hous and scholl for lasses in Montrose ; to hir I was welcome againe as her awin sone. The maister of the scholl, a lerned, honest, kynd man, whom also for thankfulnes I name, Mr Andro Miln [Minister of Fedresso][5] ; he was verie skilfull and diligent. The first yeir he causit us go throw the Rudiments againe, thairefter enter and pas throw the first part of Grammer of Sebastian ; thairwith we hard Phormionem Terentii, and war exerceisd in composition ; efter that entered to the second part, and hard thairwith the Georgics of Virgill, and dyvers uther things. I never

---

[1] Sir David Lindsay's poem *Ane Dialogue betuix Experience and ane Courteour*.
[2] beyond, more than.
[3] small farm.
[4] See p. 16.
[5] Andrew Mylne (*d.* 1605) was schoolmaster at Montrose and, after holding various charges, was presented to Fetteresso in 1579.

get a strak of his hand, whowbeit I comitted twa lurd [1] faultes, as it war with fyre and sword : Haiffing the candle in my hand on a wintar night, befor sax hours, in the scholl, sitting in the class, bernlie [2] and negligentlie pleying with the bent,[3] it kendlet sa on fyre, that we haid all ado to put it out with our feit. The uther was being molested by a condisciple, wha cutted the stringes of my pen and ink-horn with his pen-knyff, I minting [4] with my pen-knyff to his legges to fley him [5] ; he feared, and lifting now a lag, now the uther, rasht on his lag upon my knyff, and strak him selff a deipe wound in the schin of the lag, quilk was a quarter of a yeir in curing. In the tyme of the trying of this mater, he saw me sa humble, sa feared, sa greived, yeild sa manie teares, and by fasting and murning in the scholl all day, that he said he could nocht find in his hart to punishe me fordar. Bot my righteus God let me nocht slipe that fault, bot gaiff me a warning, and remember-ance what it was to be defyld with blude, whowbeit negligentlie ; for within a short space efter I haid causit a cutlar, new com to the town, to polishe and scharpe the sam pen-knyff, and haid bought a pennie-worthe of aples, and cutting and eatting the sam in the Linkes, as I put the cheive [6] in [my] mouthe, I began to lope upe upon a little sandie bray, haiffing the pen-knyff in my right hand, I fell, and thairwithe strak my selff, missing my wombe, an inche deipe in the inwart syde of the left knie, even to the bean,[7] wherby the æquitie of God's judgment and my conscience strak me sa, that I was the mair war of knyffes all my days.

In Montrose was Mr Thomas Andersone,[8] minister, a man of mean gifts, bot of singular guid lyff. God moved him to mark me, and call me often to his chalmer

---

[1] stupid.   [2] in childish fashion.
[3] It was usual to cover the stone or earthen floors with the coarse grass called " bent " in Scotland.
[4] aiming.   [5] frighten.   [6] slice.   [7] bone.
[8] Thomas Anderson (d. 1585), a former schoolmaster, was admitted to Montrose in 1566.

to treat me, when he saw anie guid in me, and to instruct and admonish me utherwayes. He desyrit me ever to rehearse a part of Calvin's Catechisme on the Sabothes at efternoone, because he hard the peiple lyked weill of the clearnes of my voice, and pronuncing with sum feiling ; and thairby God moved a godlie honest matron in the town to mak mikle of me thairfor, and called me hir lytle sweit angle. The minister was able to teatche na ofter but annes in the ouk [1] ; but haid a godlie honest man reidar [Jhone Beatie], wha read the Scripture distinctlie, and with a religius and devot feilling ; wherby I fand my selff movit to giff guid eare, and lern the Stories of Scripture, also to tak plesure in the Psalmes, quhilk he haid almost all by hart, in prose. The Lard of Done,[2] mentioned befor, dwelt oft in the town, and of his charitie interteined a blind man, wha haid a singular guid voice ; him he causit the doctor of our scholl teatche the wholl Psalmes in miter, with the tones thairof, and sing tham in the kirk ; be heiring of whome I was sa delyted, that I lernit manie of the Psalmes and toones thairof in miter, quhilk I haiff thought ever sen syne [3] a grait blessing and comfort. The exerceisc of the ministerie was keipit ouklie then in Montrose, and thair assemblies ordinarlie ; quhilk when I saw I was movit to lyk fellon [4] weill of that calling, bot thought it a thing unpossible that ever I could haiff the abilitie to stand upe and speak when all helde thair toung and luiked, and to continow speaking alean the space of an houre. Ther was also ther a post [5] [John Finheavin], that frequented Edinbruche, and brought ham Psalme buikes and ballates ; namlie, of Robert Semple's [6] making, wherin I tuik pleasour, and lernit sum thing bathe of the esteat of the countrey, and of the missours [7]

---

[1] once in the week. [2] See p. 18. [3] since that time.
[4] This word is used as a superlative—thus, " fellon weill " means exceedingly well.
[5] carrier.
[6] Robert Sempill (1530 ?-1595), a supporter of the Reformers and a writer of ballads about contemporary events. [7] measures.

and cullors of Scottes ryme. He schew me first Wedderburn's Songs,[1] wharof I lerned diverse *par ceur*, with
great diversitie of toones. He frequented our scholl,
and of him also I lerned to understand the Calender,
efter the commoun use thairof.

And, finalie, I receavit the comunion of the bodie
and blud of the Lord Jesus Chryst first at Montrose,
with a graitter reverence and sence, in my saull, then
oft thairefter I could find, in the 13 year of my age ;
whar, coming from the table, a guid honest man, ane
eldar of the kirk [Richart Andersone, brother to the
former, Mr Thomas Andersone], gaiff me an admonition
concerning lightnes, wantonnes, and nocht takin tent to [2]
the preatching and word read, and prayers, quhilk
remeaned with me ever sen syne. Sa God maid everie
persone, place, and action, to be my teatchers ; bot,
alas ! I used tham never sa fruitfullie, as the guid
occasiones servit, bot was caried away in vanitie of
mynd with young and fullishe conceattes, quhilk is the
heavie challange of my conscience. The tyme of my
being in Montrose was about twa yeirs, during the
quhilk the comoun newes that I hard was of the grait
praises of the government [3] ; and, in end, the heavie
mean [4] and pitiful regrat, amangs men in all esteatts,
for the traiterus murdour of James Earl of Murro, called
the Guid Regent, anent the quhilk, sie the 19 book of the
fornamed Cornicle.[5]

STUDENT AT ST ANDREWS

The esteat of Montrose schol changit, be occasion of
the master's taking of him to the ministerie, I cam hame

---

[1] *The Gude and Godlie Ballatis*, written by the brothers Wedderburn of
Dundee.

[2] paying attention to.

[3] James Stewart, Earl of Moray (natural son of James V), was Regent
from 1567 till January 1570, when he was assassinated. He took effective
measures to ensure prompt and full payment of the stipends of the reformed
ministers.

[4] moaning.   [5] Buchanan's History, see below, p. 30.

to Baldowy about the Lambes,[1] *in anno* 1571. The fourtein yeir of my age, now expyred, whar my father setts me about the hervest-labour, wherin I haid little pleasour ; for whowbeit I spendit nocht the tyme sa fructfullie as I might at scholl, yet I lyked the schollar's lyff best ; bot my father held us in sic aw, that we durst nocht reasone with him, bot his will was neidfull obedience to us. Sa to the glorie of my God, I remember a certean day my father send me to the smeddy [2] for dressing of hewkes [3] and sum yron instruments, the way lying hard by Mariekirk, wherin my father pretched, I begoude [4] to weirie soar of my lyff ; and as my coustome haid bein fra my bernheid to pray in my hart, and mein [5] my esteat to my God, coming fornent [6] the kirk, and luiking to it, the Lord steirit upe an extraordinar motion in my hart, quhilk maid me atteans,[7] being alean, to fall on gruiff [8] to the ground, and pour out a schort and ernest petition to God, that it wald please his guidnes to offer occasion to continow me at the scholles, and inclyne my father's hart till use the saming [9] ; with promise and vow, that whatever missour [10] of knawlage and letters he wold bestow on me, I sould, by his grace, imploy the saming for his glorie in the calling of the ministerie ; and rysing from the ground with joy and grait contentment in hart, again fell downe and worschipped, and sa past on and did the earand, retourning and praising my God, singing sum Psalmes. Within a few dayes thairefter, Mr James Melvill, my uncle,[11] comes to Baldowy, and brings with him a godlie lernit man, named Mr Wilyeam Collace,[12] wha was that

[1] Lammas, 1st August.   [2] smithy.   [3] reaping hooks.   [4] began.
[5] bemoan.   [6] opposite.   [7] at once.   [8] flat, prostrate.
[9] same.   [10] measure.   [11] See p. 18.
[12] In 1574 (after Andrew Melville's return home) James Melville notes : " Nocht lang efter Mr Andro receavit letters from Monsieur du Bez, and therin amangs the rest, ' Colaceus vester, exemplar omnium virtutum, nuper apud nos vita functus est.' This was my guid regent, wha, efter the ending of our course, haid gean to France, and coming to Genev, ther died ; a grait los to the Kirk of God in his countrey, for he was solidlie lernit, hailelie addicted to divinitie, with a sincear and zealus hart."

sam yeir to tak upe the class as first regent of St Leonard's Collage, within the Universitie of St Andros ; efter conference with whome that night, God moves my father's hart to resolve to send me that sam yeir to the Collage. Trew it was, I was bot weaklie groundit in grammar, and young of yeirs ; yit the lovingnes of the gentleman, and promise of the benefeit of a bursare's place, and of taking peanes on me, maid the mater to go fordwart ; wherof, when I was informed be my said uncle, and haid sein and spoken a lytle with the man, Rebecca was never blyther to go with the servant of Abraham, nor I was to go with him. And trewlie this finding of God, at a neid, was the beginning of a ritche treassour of the pruiff of his providence, mercie, and grace, continowallie increassing sen syne, that I wald nocht giff for ten thowsand warlds.

Sa I cam to St Androis about the first of November, in the forsaid yeir 1571,[1] and enterit in the course of Philosophie, under the regenterie [2] of the said Mr Wilyeam, wha haid the estimation of the maist solide and lernit in Aristotle's Philosophie. And first hard under him Cassander his Rhetorik ; but at the beginning, nather being weill groundet in grammer, nor com to the yeirs of naturall judgment and understanding, I was cast in sic a greiff and dispear, because I understood nocht the regent's langage in teatching, that I did nathing bot bursted and grat [3] at his lessones, and was of mynd to haiff gone ham agean, war nocht the luiffing cear of that man comforted me, and tuik me in his awin chalmer, causit me ly with him selff, and everie night teatched me in privat, till I was acquented with the mater. [We hard the Oration, Pro Rege Deiotaro.] Then he gaiff us a compend of his awin of Philosophi

---

[1] This (as are other dates relating to Melville's University course) is wrong. The records of St Andrews University show that he matriculated in 1569 and was admitted Bachelor of Arts in 1572. There are also other chronological errors (see notes on following pages).

[2] A regent took a class through its entire Arts course.

[3] burst into tears.

and the partes thairof; of Dialectik, of Definition, of Division, of Enunciation, and of a Syllogisme Enthymen, and Induction, &c.; quhilk I thought I understuid better. About the quhilk tyme my father coming to the town, begoude to examine me, and finding sum beginning was exceidinglie rejoysit, and uttered sweittar affection to me then ever before. He interteined my regent verie hartlie in his ludging, and gaiff him grait thanks. He send me to him, efter he haid taken leive, with twa piece of gold in a neapkine; bot the gentleman was sa honest and loving, that he wald haiff non of his gold, but with austere countenance send me bak with it, na never wald receave gold nor silver all the tyme of my course. We enterit in the Organ of Aristotle's Logics that yeir, and lernit till the Demonstrations. He haid a lytle boy that servit him in his chamber, called David Elistone, wha, amangs threttie-and-sax schollars in number, (sa manie war we in the class,) was the best. This boy he causit weat on me, and confer with me; whase ingyne and judgment past me als far in the wholl course of philosophie, as the aigle the howlet.[1] In the multiplication of Propositiones, Medalles, Conversion of Syllogismes, Pons Asinorum, etc., he was als read as I was in telling an-and-threttie.[2] This I mark for a speciall cause of thankfulnes following.

A GLIMPSE OF JOHN KNOX

Bot of all the benefites I haid that yeir[3] was the coming of that maist notable profet and apostle of our nation, Mr Jhone Knox, to St Androis; wha, be the faction of the Quein occupeing the castell and town of Edinbruche, was compellit to remove thairfra with a number of the best, and chusit to com to St Androis. I hard him teatche ther the prophecie of Daniel that simmer,

[1] as the eagle the owl.
[2] as ready as I was in counting to one-and-thirty.
[3] 1571.

and the wintar following. I haid my pen and my litle book, and tuk away sic things as I could comprehend. In the opening upe of his text he was moderat the space of an halff houre ; bot when he enterit to application, he maid me sa to grew [1] and tremble, that I could nocht hald a pen to wryt. I hard him oftymes utter these thretenings in the hicht of their pryde, quhilk the eis [2] of monie saw cleirlie brought to pass within few yeirs upon the Captean of that Castle,[3] the Hamiltones,[4] and the Quein hir selff. He ludgit down in the Abbay besyde our Collage ; and our [Primarius, Mr James Wilkie,[5] our] Regents, Mr Nicol Dalgleise,[6] Mr Wilyeam Colace,[7] and Mr Jhone Davidsone,[8] went in ordinarlie to his grace efter denner and soupper. Our Regent taried all the vacans [9] to heir him, whowbeit he haid urgent effeares of his brother-sonnes to handle, to whom he was tutor. Mr Knox wald sum tymes com in and repose him in our Collage yeard, and call us schollars unto him and bless us, and exhort us to knaw God and his wark in our contrey, and stand be the guid cause, to use our tyme weill, and lern the guid instructiones, and follow the guid exemple of our maisters. Our haill Collage, maisters and schollars, war sound and zelus for the guid cause.

[1] shudder.
[2] eyes.
[3] William Kirkcaldy of Grange, at one time a supporter of the Reformers, held Edinburgh Castle for Queen Mary from 1568 to 1573 when he surrendered and was executed (see p. 35).
[4] See p. 27.
[5] James Wilkie (1512-1590), a former Regent at St Leonard's, was appointed Principal in 1570. In 1578 he was admitted minister of St Leonard's Church, holding the charge in conjunction.
[6] Nicol Dalgleish (*d.* 1608) became minister of St Cuthbert's in Edinburgh in 1581. He was admitted to Pittenweem in 1589 (see p. 9).
[7] See p. 23.
[8] John Davidson (1549-1604) was imprisoned for a poem derogatory to Morton, and on his release went to the Continent. He returned in 1577 and became minister of Liberton in 1579 and of Prestonpans in 1595.
[9] vacation.

A LIBERAL EDUCATION

The second yeir of my course,[1] we hard the Demonstrations, the Topiks, and the Sophist Captiones. And the Primarius [Mr James Wilkie], a guid, peacable, sweit auld man, wha luiffed me weill, teached the four speaces of the Arithmetik, and sum thing of the Sphere ; bot the graittest benefit I had of him was his daylie doctrine at the prayers in the kirk, everie morning ; for he past throw the twa buiks of Samuel, and twa of the Kings, very pleanlie and substantiuslie, quhilk I rememberit the better ever since. He causit sing comounlie the 44 and 79 Psalmes, quhilk I lernit *par ceur*, for that was the yeir of the bludie massacres in France, and grait troubles in this countrey, the warres betwix Leithe and Edinbruche being verie hat. The Castel of Dumbarten was notablie tean,[2] and Jhone Hamilton, Bischope of St Androis, hangit.[3]

In the moneth of August,[4] " the Blak Parliament " of Stirling haldin [The parliament was haldin in August 1571, before I cam to the Universitie.], whar the second Regent[5] was slean, in Wolmistones armes, &c., vide Buchan. Chro.

The thrid yeir[6] of our course, we hard the fyve buikis of the Ethiks, with the aught buikis of the Physiks, [and *De Ortu et Interitu.*] That yeir we haid our Bachlar art,[7] according to the solemnities then used of declama-

---

[1] 1572 is the date given by Melville (see note on p. 24).
[2] taken. This happened in May 1571.
[3] At Stirling, 7th April 1571, for complicity in the murders of Darnley and of the Regent Moray.   [4] 1571.
[5] Matthew Stewart, fourth Earl of Lennox, shot during a skirmish on 4th September 1571.
[6] 1573 is the date given by Melville (see note on p. 24).
[7] In his third session a student proceeded to his Bachelor's degree. He had to pass certain tests (the " declamations " mentioned by Melville) and he had to give a banquet. In his fourth year he had to pass more tests, for one of which he was seated on the " black stone," and he was then admitted Master of Arts and received a licence to teach anywhere in Christendom. Another of these fourth-year tests was known as the " vikis," a colloquialism for " responsiones in vico," a phrase borrowed from Paris where the Faculty Schools were in the Vicus Stramineus.

tions, banqueting, and playes. And in the mean tyme thairof, my father maried my said eldest sistar Isbell, and second, Marjorie, bathe on a day ; bot efter that festing, we gat hard newes of the defeat of the Forbesses at the Crabstean, besyd Aberdein.[1]

The fourt and last yeir of our course,[2] quhilk was the 17 yeir of my age outpast, and 18 rinning, we lerned the buikis de Cœlo and Mateors, also the Spher, more exactlie teachit be our awin Regent, and maid us for our Vicces and Blakstens,[3] and haid at Pace [4] our promotion and finissing of our course. The beginning of this yeir was also maist dulfull to me, by the departour of my deirest sistar Isbell, wha died of hir first bern ; in whom I lossit my naturall mother the second tyme.

In the thrid and fourt yeirs of my course, at the direction of my father, I hard the Comissar, Mr Wilyeam Skein, teatche Cicero de Legibus, and divers partes of the Institutiones of Justinian. I was burdet in the hous of a man of law, a very guid honest man, Andro Greine be nam, wha lovit me exceiding weill ; whase wyff also was ane of my mothers. I am sure sche haid nocht sone nor bern sche loved better. This lawier tuk me to the Consistorie [5] with him, whar the Comissar wald tak pleasour to schaw us the practise, in judgment, of that quhilk he teatched in the scholles. He was a man of skill and guid conscience in his calling, lernit and diligent in his profession, and tuk delyt in na thing mair nor to repeat ower and ower again to anie schollar that wald ask him the thingis he haid bein teatching. Lykwayes my ost, Andro, acquentit me with the formes of summonds and lybelling, of contracts, obligatiounes, actes, &c. ; but my hart was nocht sett that way.

---

[1] The Master of Forbes, the King's deputy in the north, was defeated and captured by the Gordons in 1571. Control of the north thus passed to the Catholic or Queen's Party.

[2] 1574 is the date given by Melville (see note on p. 24).

[3] See note on p. 27.   [4] Easter (Pasch).

[5] The Reformation put an end to the Consistorial Courts, but in 1563 Commissary Courts were established for much the same purposes.

Mairower, in these yeirs I lerned my music, wherin I tuk graitter delyt, of an [1] Alexander Smithe, servant to the Primarius of our Collage, wha haid been treaned upe amangis the mounks in the Abbay. I lerned of him the gam,[2] plean-song, and monie of the treables of the Psalmes, wherof sum I could weill sing in the kirk ; bot my naturalitie and easie lerning by the ear maid me the mair unsolide and unreadie to use the forme of the art. I lovit singing and playing on instruments passing weill, and wald gladlie spend tyme whar the exerceise thairof was within the Collage ; for twa or thrie of our condisciples played fellon weill on the virginals, and another on the lut and githorn.[3] Our Regent haid also the pinalds [4] in his chalmer, and lernit some thing, and I eftir him ; bot perceaving me ower mikle caried efter that, he dishanted [5] and left of. It was the grait mercie of my God that keipit me from anie grait progress in singing and playing on instruments ; for, giff I haid atteined to anie reasonable missure thairin, I haid never don guid utherwayes, in respect of my amorus disposition, wherby Sathan sought even then to deboiche me ; bot my God gaiff me a piece of his fear, and grait naturall shamfastness, quhilk by his grace war my preservatives. Als I haid my necessars honestlie aneuche of my father, bot nocht els ; for archerie and goff, I haid bow, arrose, glub and bals, but nocht a purs for catchpull [6] and tavern ; sic was his fatherlie wisdom for my weill. Yit now and then I lernit and usit sa mikle bathe of the hand and racket catche as might serve for moderat and halsome exerceise of the body.

I wald haiff gladlie bein at the Greik and Hebrew toungs, because I red in our Byble that it was translated out of Hebrew and Greik ; bot the langages war nocht to be gottine in the land. Our Regent begoud and teatched us the A, B, C, of the Greik, and the simple declintiones, bot went no farder. Be that occasion he

---

[1] one.   [2] gamut.   [3] guitar.   [4] spinet.
[5] abandoned.   [6] a game akin to fives.

tauld me of my uncle Mr Andro Melvill, whom he knew
in the tyme of his course in the New Collage to use the
Greik Logics of Aristotle ; quhilk was a wounder to
tham that he was sa fyne a schollar, and of sic expectation.
This maid me inquyre for Mr Andro, when I cam ham,
the second and thrid yeir of our course ; bot my father
and Mr James schew me they fearit he was dead, because
of the grait civill warres in France, and that they hard
he was in Poictears beseiged ; that it was aught or nyne
yeirs sen he past to France, and four or fyve yeirs sen
they gat anie letters or word from him. This twitched
my hart wounder soar,[1] in respect of the grait comendation
I hard of him be my Regent and diverse uthers. Bot
soon efter, about the middes of our thrid yeir, Alexander
Young [2] cam ham from Genev, from his uncle, and my
neir kinsman, Mr Henrie Scrymgour,[3] of honourable
memorie, with sum propynes [4] to the King, and letters
to Mr George Bowchanan [5] and Mr Piter Young,[6] that
an the King's maister, that uther his pædagog ; and
amangs the rest brought letters from the said Mr Andro
to my father, and his brother Mr James ; and thair-
withall word of his weilfear and singular estimation in
Genev, whar he haid four yeirs professit. Of these newes
my hart was exceiding glade, and the said Alexander

---

[1] touched my heart wonderfully sore.

[2] Alexander Young, brother of Peter Young (see note 6), was sent to
Geneva in 1572 by Regent Mar and George Buchanan to ask his uncle
Henry Scrymgeour (see note 3) to return home.

[3] Henry Scrymgeour (1506-1572) graduated at St Andrews in 1534
and then went to the Continent, eventually becoming Professor of Civil
Law at Geneva. He was a man of great learning. Scrymgeour was
probably a brother of the mother of James Melville and of the mother of
Alexander and Peter Young.

[4] presents.

[5] George Buchanan (1506-1582), the famous historian and scholar,
was tutor to James VI from 1570 to 1578. Melville frequently refers to his
Rerum Scoticarum Historia.

[6] Peter Young (1544-1628) shared with George Buchanan the oversight
of the education of James VI (according to McCrie, Young attended
" to the more trivial parts of the instruction "). He became one of the
King's favourite counsellors.

being with all diligence to return againe to Genev, I haid a letter in readines pennit at lainthe in Latin, the best I could, quhilk I delyverit to my cowsing Alexander, wha within a twa monethes put it in the hands of my said uncle Mr Andro. And he tauld me at meitting, and oft sen syne, it was a speciall motion of his hamcoming, then the quhilk, I, nor Scotland nather, receavit never a graitter benefit of the hands of God, as will better appeir heirefter.

Bot because, in all my course, the graittest benefit was the sight and heiring of that extraordinar man of God, Mr Jhone Knox ; sa far as I then knew and hard of him, I man heir record. In the tyme of his being in St Androis,[1] ther was a General Assemblie hauldin in the scholles of St Leonards, our Collage. Thair, amangs uther things, was motioned the making of Bischopes ; to the quhilk Mr Knox opponit him selff directlie and zealuslie. Yit a number of Commissionars of the Kirk, meatt at Leithe,[2] with the Lords that haid the guid caus in hand, (wharof everie ane was hounting for a fatt kirk leiving, quhilk gart them feght the fastar,) and ther aggreit to mak Bischopes ; the warst turn that ever was done for the kirk leiving, as experience atteanes declared, when they war named " Tulchains," that is, calffs' skinnes stuffed with stra, to cause the cow giff milk ; for everie lord gat a bischoprie, and sought and presented to the kirk sic a man as wald be content with least, and sett tham maist of fewes, takes,[3] and pensiones. Amangs the rest, the Erle of Mortoun gat the bischoprik of St Androis, efter the hanging of Jhone Hamiltone[4] ; and presented therunto that honorable father of the Universitie, as Rector thairof for the present, Mr Jhone

[1] See p. 25 above.
[2] The Convention of Leith met on 12th January 1572—the General Assembly at St Andrews on 6th March 1572. Melville has this correctly in a marginal note.
[3] tacks, leases.
[4] See p. 27 above.

Dowglass,[1] a guid, upright-harted man, bot ambitius and simple, nocht knawing wha delt with him. I hard Mr Knox speak against it, bot sparinglie, because he lovit the man ; and with regrat, saying, " Alas ! for pitie, to lay upone an auld weak man's back that quhilk twentie of the best gifts could nocht bear. It will wrak him and disgrace him ! " And, indeid, it cam to pass sa ; for within twa or thrie yeirs he died ; during the quhilk he haid nather that honour, welthe, nor helthe, as he was wount to haiff, ever repenting that he tuk it on. That was the first tyme I hard Mr Patrik Constantine,[2] wha, then new retourned out of France with young Mr James Macgill, the Clark Register eldest sone, thought, be the said Clark's court, wha was grait with the Erle of Mortoun, to haiff bein preferrit to the bischoprik, bot coming schort, becam a zealus preatchour against Bischopes. I hard a sermont of his the ouk efter the Bischope was maid, upon ane extraordinar day, that he might haiff the graitter audience ; wherin he maid thrie sorts of Bischoppes : My Lord Bischop, My Lord's Bischop, and The Lord's Bischope. " My Lord Bischope," said he, " was in the Papistrie : My Lord's Bischope is now, when my Lord getts the benefice, and the Bischope serves for na thing bot to mak his tytle sure : And The Lord's Bischope is the trew Minister of the Gospell." Mr Patrik was then weill lyked, and of guid expectation

---

[1] John Douglas (*d.* 1574) was a kinsman of Regent Morton and was Principal of St Mary's College, St Andrews, when he was promoted to the Archbishopric in 1571. He was a man of great scholarship and piety, but was merely a tool in the hands of Morton, who drew the greater part of the income of the see.

[2] Patrick Adamson (see note on p. 47) inherited two patronymics— Adamson and Constantine (or Constant or Coustan). Like his ancestors he was called sometimes by one and sometimes by the other. He was born in 1536, took his degree at St Andrews in 1558, and was admitted minister of Ceres in 1560. In 1564 the General Assembly refused to grant him permission to go to France " for augmenting of his knowledge," but he resigned his charge and went to the Continent as tutor to the eldest son of Sir James Macgill, Clerk Register. He returned in 1570, practised as an advocate for two years, and in 1572 became minister of Paisley.

with sic as knew him nocht intus.[1] The yeir efter was maid Bischope, Geordie of Murro,[2] whom I saw a haill wintar mumling on his pretching af his peapers everie day at our morning prayers ; and haid it nocht weill *par ceur* when all was done : And efter him, Bischope Patone of Dunkell.[3] [I saw them bathe gett imposition of hands be B. Douglas and Mr Jhon Woundrom,[4] Superintendent, whom I saw inaugarat (as they cald it) B. Douglas.] This grievit the hart of the man of God to the dead ; bot the warres war sa hatt, and the Lords cryed they behud [5] to leave tham, giff they gatt nocht the kirk leiving ; and monie knew nocht yit the corruption and unlawfulness of that invention of men, and sa the mater past fordwart.

At Mr Knox coming to St Androis, Robert Lekprivik, printar, transported his lettres and press from Edinbruch to St Androis, whar first I saw that excellent art of printing ; and haid then in hand Mr Patrik Constant's Catechisme of Calvin,[6] converted in Latin heroic vers, quhilk with the author was mikle estimed of.

MORE ABOUT JOHN KNOX

The town of Edinbruche recovered againe, and the guid and honest men therof retourned to thair housses. Mr Knox with his familie past hame to Edinbruche.[7] Being in St Androis he was verie weak. I saw him everie day of his doctrine go hulie and fear,[8] with a furring of

[1] inwardly.
[2] George Douglas (*d.* 1589), natural son of the sixth Earl of Angus, became Bishop of Moray in 1573.
[3] James Paton (*c.* 1520-1596), minister of Muckhart from 1567 to 1572 when he became Bishop of Dunkeld. He was supposed to have supported Huntly and the other papist earls and was excommunicated in 1582.
[4] John Wynram (1492-1582), appointed Superintendent of Fife in 1560 and of Strathern in 1572.
[5] behoved.
[6] Patrick Constantine's or Adamson's (see pp. 32 and 47) *Catechismus Latino Carmine Redditus*.
[7] Knox returned to Edinburgh in August 1572.
[8] " Hulie " or " hooly " means " slowly " and " hooly and fair " was a common adverbial phrase meaning " cautiously " or " carefully."

martriks [1] about his neck, a staff in the an hand, and guid godlie Richart Ballanden, [2] his servand, halding upe the uther oxtar, from the Abbay to the paroche kirk ; and be the said Richart and another servant, lifted upe to the pulpit, whar he behovit to lean at his first entrie ; bot or he haid done with his sermont, he was sa active and vigorus that he was lyk to ding that pulpit in blads, [3] and fly out of it ! Sa, soone efter his coming to Edinbruche, he becam unable to preatche ; and sa instituting in his roum, [4] be the ordinar calling of the kirk and congregation, Mr James Lawsone, [5] [a man of singular learning, zeal, and eloquence, whom I never hard preatche bot he meltit my hart with teares,] he tuk him to his chamber, and most happelie and comfortablie departed this lyff. Vide concerning his lyff and dathe, Mr Thomas Smeton's buik against Hamiltone the Apostat. [6]

Ther was twa in St Androis wha war his aydant [7] heirars, and wrot his sermonts ; an, my condisciple, Mr Andro Yowng, [8] now minister of Dumblean, wha transleated sum of tham in Latin, and read tham in the hall of the Collage in stead of his orations : that uther was servant to Mr Robert Hamilton, [9] minister of the

---

[1] a fur of marten.

[2] Richard Bannatyne (d. 1605) was secretary to John Knox and author of *Memorials of Transactions in Scotland from 1569 to 1573.*

[3] to thump the pulpit into bits.　　[4] in his place.

[5] James Lawson (1538-1584), fellow student of Andrew Melville at St Andrews ; taught Hebrew in New College, St Andrews, 1568 ; Sub-Principal of Aberdeen, 1569 ; called to succeed Knox in St Giles and admitted 1572. He was largely responsible for the founding of Edinburgh University.

[6] Thomas Smeaton (1536-1583), Regent in St Salvator's College, was ejected by the Reformers. He went to the Continent and became a Jesuit but eventually renounced Popery. In 1577 he became minister of Paisley, and in 1580 Principal of Glasgow University and minister of Govan. He was a scholar of distinction and a close friend of Andrew Melville. His book, *Ad Virulentum Archibaldi Hamiltonii Apostatae Dialogum . . . Orthodoxa Responsio etc.*, was published in 1579.　　[7] diligent, regular.

[8] Andrew Young held various charges before becoming minister of Dunblane in 1578, which charge he held till 1606.

[9] Robert Hamilton (d. 1581) became minister of St Andrews in 1566. He was also Regent in and then Principal of New College till 1579.

town, whom Mr Robert causit to wrait, for what end God knawes. The threatnings of his sermonts war verie soar ; and sa particular, that sic as lyket nocht the cause, tuk occasion to reprotche him as a rashe raler, without warrand. And Mr Robert Hamilton himselff being offendit, conferrit with Mr Knox, asking his warrand of that particular thretning against the Castel of Edinbruche, that it sould rin lyk a sand-glass ; it sould spew out the Captan[1] with scham ; he sould nocht com out at the yet, bot down ower the walles ; and sic lyk. Mr Knox answerit, " God is my warrant, and yie sall sie it." Whill as the uther was skarslie satisfeit, and tuk hardlie with it, the nixt sermont from pulpit, he repeates the thretnings, and addes therto, " Thow, that will nocht beleive my warrand, sall sie it with thy eis that day ; and sall say, What haif I to do heir ? " This sermont the said Mr Robert's servand wrot ; and, being with his maister in Edinbruche a twa yeir thairefter, at the taking of the Castell, they ged[2] upe to the Castell-hill, saw the forwark of the Castell all demolished, and rinning lyk a sandie bray ; they saw the men of wear all sett in ordour ; the Captan, with a lytle cut of a staff in his hand, takin doun ower the wall upon the leathers[3] ; and Mr Robert, troublet with the thrang[4] of the peiple, sayes to this man, " Go, what haif I ado heir ? " And, in going away, the servant remembers his maister of that sermont, and the words ; wha was compellit to glorifie God, and say, he was a trew prophet.

ANDREW MELVILLE COMES HOME AND TAKES HIS NEPHEW IN HAND

Thus, ending my course of Philosophie in St Androis, whar upon the part of God I haid offerit to me all guid

---

[1] See p. 26. [2] went. [3] ladders.
[4] crowd or, perhaps, pressure of the crowd.

occasion of godlines, lerning, and wesdome, sa mikle as was in the countrey for the tyme, [and might fall in my age ;] bot on my part, wha throw wantones and vanitie neglected and mispent the occasiones, haid gottin na thing bot a nam and opinion of lerning, a babling of words without wit, at least wesdome : For my light young nature was giffen mair to be superficiall nor solid, circumferentiall nor centrik, desyring to heir and haiff the names of manie things, bot never weill degesting nor ryping [1] out the nature of anie, bot fleiting and flowing, soon lyking and soon lothing everie thing. Onlie now and then I fand sum sweit and constant motiones of the feir and love of God within me.

I cam to Dondie, whar my uncle Roger,[2] a man godlie, kynd, and wyse, enterit with me to understand to what calling my hart inclyned ; and gaiff out that my father's intention was to haiff me a lawer. I said nocht mikle against it, bot wissed at God I might haiff the gifts and grace to be a minister. Coming ham, my father tented [3] me in the sam maner, bot nocht sa familiarlie ; nather durst I utter anie thing against his opinion and judgment, bot said I was readie to obey his will and direction in all things. He commandit me then to occupie my tyme weill amangs his books till the vacans, at what tyme he wald haiff occasion to meit with sum guid man of law in Edinbruche, to whom he wald put me in service. Giff sa he meinde, indeid, because he saw na provision for the ministerie, or to essay my resolution, I can nocht tell. Going a day to Bonitone, I past by the Kirk of Maritone and place wher I haid prayed, and vowed to God [4] : the sam cam in my memorie, with a grait motion of mynd and determination to pay my vow, giff God wald giff the

---

[1] searching.

[2] " Roger, burgess of Dondie, a man of singular giftes of nature and God's grace, bot was nocht traned upe in lettres " (MS.). " I haiff hard Mr Robert Bruce say oft of Roger, that giff he haid haid Mr Andro's lerning, he wald be the oddest man in Europe " (margin of MS.).

[3] sounded.   [4] See p. 23 above.

grace and moyen.[1] Sa, praying and worschiping befor
God, it cam in my mynd to pen a sermont upon a part
of Scripture, and leave it in a buik of my father, whar
he might find it ; and sa I tuk the beginning of the
nynt of Jhone's Evangell, of the blind man, and studeing
his comentares thairon, Musculus and Marlorot, wrot
it and left it in Musculus' Comentars ; quhilk, when
he fand it, lyked him weill ; yit spak na thing, bot left
me in suspence till it pleasit God to giff me full resolution.
For, a lytle befor Lambes, word cam that Mr Andro
was com to Edinbruche, and within twentie dayes efter
he cam to Baldowy ; with whom when my father had
conferit, and knawin what opinion he haid of me, he
delyverit me ower unto him, thinking he was disburdenit
of me ; and sa indeid he was, as the continuation of this
narrative will declar. This was in the yeir of God 1574.

Sa he cam to Baldowy to his brother, my father, whar
he remeaned that hervest quarter, and whar, within a
few dayes efter his coming, I was resigned ower be my
father hailelie unto him to veak upon him [2] as his sone
and servant ; and, as my father said to him, to be a
pladge of his love. And surlie his service was easie,
nocht to me onlie, bot even to the fremdest man [3] that
ever served him ; for he schosed for his servantes onlie
schollars, and giff they haid done anie guid at thair
book, he cared nocht what they did to him. That
quarter of yeir I thought I gat graitter light in letters
nor all my tyme befor ; whowbeit at our meitting, in
my conceat I thought I could haiff taked to him in
things I haid hard, as he did to me as a Maister of Arts ;
bot I perceavit at annes that I was bot an ignorant
bable, and wist nocht what I said, nather could schaw
anie use thairof, bot in clattering and crying. He fand
me bauche [4] in the Latin toung, a pratler upon precepts

---

[1] means.
[2] to wait upon his leisure.
[3] the greatest stranger.
[4] deficient.

in Logik without anie profit for the right use, and
haiffing sum termes of Art in Philosophie without light
of solid knawlage ; yit of ingyne and capacitie guid
aneuche, wherby I haid cunned [1] my *dictata*, and haid
them readie aneuche. He enterit thairfor and conferrit
with me sum of Bowchanan's Psalmes, of Virgill and
Horace ; quhilk twa, namlie Virgill, was his cheiff
refreschment efter his grave studies ; wherin he lut me
sie, nocht onlie the proper Latin langage and ornaments
of poesie, bot also mair guid Logik and Philosophie then
ever I haid hard befor. I had tean delyt at the Grammer
Schole to heir reid and sung the verses of Virgill, taken
with the numbers thairof, (whowbeit I knew nocht what
numbers was till he tauld me,) and haid mikle of him
par ceur ; bot I understud never a lyne of him till then.
He read a comedie of Tyrence with me, schawing me
that ther was bathe fyne Latin langage and wit to be
lernit : That of langage I thought weill, bot for wit I
merveled, and haid nocht knawin befor. He put in my
hand the Comentares of Cæsar, comending him for the
simple puritie of the Latin toung ; also Salust, and
read with me the Conjuration of Catelin. He haid
gottin in Paris, at his by-coming, Bodin his Method of
Historie, quhilk he read ower him selff thryse or four
tymes that quarter, annes with me, and the rest whill
I was occupied in the Greik grammer, quhilk he put in
hand, of Clenard ; causing me understand the precepts
onlie, and lear the παραδειγματα exactlie ; the practise
wharof he schew me in my buik, going throw with me
that Epistle of Basilius, and cawsing me lern it be hart,
bathe for the langage and the mater. Thairefter to the
New Testament, and ged throw sum chapters of Mathew,
and certean confortable places of the Epistles, namlie
the Romans. And last, entering to the Hebrew, I gat
the reiding declynations and pronons, and sum also of
the conjugations out of Martinius' Grammer, quhilk he
haid with him, and schew me the use of the Dictionair

[1] learned.

also, quhilk he haid of Reuclius with him. And all this,
as it war, bot pleying and craking [1]; sa that I lernit
mikle mair by heiring of him in daylie conversation,
bathe that quarter and thairefter, nor ever I lernit of anie
buik ; whowbeit he set me ever to the best authors.

ANDREW MELVILLE AS PRINCIPAL OF GLASGOW UNIVERSITY

We cam to Glasgw about the first of November 1574,
whare we fand Mr Piter Blakburn,[2] a guid man, new
com from St Androis, enterit in the Collage, and begoun
to teatche conform to the ordour of the course of St
Androis. But Mr Andro, entering principall maister,
all was committed and submitted to him ; wha permitted, willinglie, to the said Mr Piter the cair of the
Collage leiving, quhilk was but verie small, consisting
in litle annualles [3] then ; and set him haillelie to teatche
things nocht hard in this countrey of befor, wherin he
travelit [4] exceiding diligentlie, as his delyt was thairin
alleanerlie.[5] Sa falling to wark with a few number of
capable heirars, sic as might be instructars of uthers
thairefter, he teatched tham the Greik grammer, the
Dialectic of Ramus, the Rhetoric of Taleus, with the
practise thairof in Greik and Latin authors, namlie,
Homer, Hesiod, Phocilides, Theognides, Pythagoras,
Isocrates, Pindarus, Virgill, Horace, Theocritus, &c.
From that he enterit to the Mathematiks, and teatched
the Elements of Euclid, the Arithmetic and Geometrie
of Ramus, the Geographie of Dyonisius, the Tables of
Hunter, the Astrologie of Aratus. From that to the
Morall Philosophie ; he teatched the Ethiks of Aristotle,

[1] chatting.
[2] Peter Blackburn (d. 1616), educated at St Andrews ; Regent in
Glasgow 1574-1582 ; minister of West Church, Aberdeen, 1582-1596, and
of East Church, 1596-1600 ; Bishop of Aberdeen, 1600.
[3] small annual payments.
[4] worked.
[5] exclusively.

the Offices of Cicero, Aristotle de Virtutibus, Cicero's
Paradoxes, and Tusculanes, Aristot. Polyb. and certean
of Platoes Dialoges. From that to the Naturall
Philosophie ; he teatched the buiks of the Physics,
De Ortu, De Cœlo, &c., also of Plato and Fernelius.
With this he joyned the Historie, with the twa lights
thairof, Chronologie and Chirographie,[1] out of Sleidan,
Menarthes, and Melancthon. And all this, by and
attoure [2] his awin ordinar profession, the holie tonges
and Theologie ; he teachit the Hebrew grammar, first
schortlie, and syne mor accuratlie ; thairefter the Caldaic
and Syriac dialects, with the practise thairof in the
Psalmes and warks of Solomon, David, Ezra, and Epistle
to the Galates. He past throw the haill comoun places
of Theologie verie exactlie and accuratlie ; also throw
all the Auld and New Testament. And all this in the
space of sax yeirs ; during the quhilk he teatchit everie
day, customablie, twyse, Sabothe and uther day ; with
an ordinar conference with sic as war present efter denner
and supper. His lerning and peanfulnes [3] was mikle
admired, sa that the nam of that Collage within twa
yeirs was noble throwout all the land, and in uther
countreys also. Sic as haid passed ther course in St
Androis cam in nomber ther, and entered schollars
again under ordour and discipline, sa that the Collage
was sa frequent [4] as the roumes war nocht able to receave
tham. The scolmaister of the town, Mr Patrik Scharpe,
was his ordinar heirar and contubernall,[5] whome he
instructed, and directed in the maist commodius bringing
upe of the youthe in grammer and guid authors ; whom
I hard oftentymes profes that he lerned mair of Mr Andro
Melvill craking and pleying, for understanding of the
authors quhilk he teatched in the scholl, nor be all his
comentares. Sic lyk Mr Piter Blackburn,[6] wha tuk upe

[1] handwriting.
[2] over and above.
[3] painstaking methods.
[4] so much frequented.
[5] companion. Patrick Sharp (d. 1615), master of the Grammar
School of Glasgow, became Principal of the University in 1585.
[6] See p. 39.

the first clas. Finalie, I dar say ther was na place in Europe comparable to Glasgw for guid letters, during these yeirs, for a plentifull and guid chepe mercat of all kynd of langages, artes, and sciences.

THE REGENT MORTON

This Regent, Erle of Mortoun,[1] was a man ever cast upon the best syde, and did honestlie and stoutlie in the cause. He lovit Mr Knox whill he was alyve. At his deathe and buriall he gaiff him ane honorable testimonie, " That he nather fearit nor flatterit anie fleche ! " and, efter his deathe, was frindlie to his wyff and childring. He was verie wyse, and a guid Justiciar, in administration. His fyve yeirs [2] war estimed to be als happie and peacable as ever Scotland saw. The name of a Papist durst nocht be hard of ; ther was na theiff nor oppressour that durst kythe.[3] Bot he could nocht suffer Chryst to reing [4] frielie be rebuking of sinne, bot maid opposition to the ministrie of Edinbruche in publict place ; nor be the right government of his Kirk be the Presbyterie of his lawfullie callit pastors and eldars, mislyked the Assemblies Generall, and wald haiff haid the name thairof changit, that he might abolishe the previlage and force thairof. Wharunto my uncle, Mr Andro, specialie opponit him selff, and thairby, and for the Bischops, incurrit his speciall indignation.

MR ANDREW INTERPRETS A DREAM

The Collage [5] haid monie pleyes in law depending that yeir,[6] and Mr Piter Blakburn was Œconomus and speciall actor ; yit, because the æstimation of Mr Andro

[1] James Douglas, fourth Earl of Morton, Regent of Scotland from November 1572 till March 1577-1578 ; executed in 1581 for being " art and part in concealing the King's father's murder."
[2] as regent.   [3] show himself.   [4] reign.
[5] Glasgow University.   [6] 1578.

was graitter, he desyrit him at certean peremptor dyettes to be present in Edinbruche. For sic a dyet, being to go to Edinbruche, Mr Piter comes in to his chalmer in the morning, heavie and grim-lyk. Being inquyrit be the Principall what ealed him, he answerit, " I haiff dreamed an unsall [1] dream, and I am sum thing solist [2] efter it." " What is it ? " sayes he. " Methought we war sitting at our Collage burde,[3] and a cap [4] full of barmie drink befor us. I luiked to the cap, and I thought I saw a read-headit tead lope out of it,[5] and craled upe upon the wall, the quhilk I perceved and dang down, and tramped under my feit ; and as I turned, I saw an uther lope out also, quhilk, whowbeit I followed, it gat away in a holl out of my sight." " Be nocht solist," sayes he, " Mr Piter ; I will interpret your dream, and warrand the interpretation trew, for a pynt of wyne ! "—" For suthe," sayes the uther, " and it be guid, a quart ! "— " The Collage burd and cap is our Collage leiving, into the quhilk twa read-nebbit [6] teades hes intrusit thamselff. They ar the twa read-neased Compeditours [7] of our Collage, against the quhilk yie haiff presentlie the actiones, viz. Jhone Grame, the first whom yie persewing at this dyet, clim als weill as he will on the wall of the law, yie sall ding down and owercome. The uther is the read-faced Commissar, Mr Archbald Beaton, wha be some wyll sall eschew presentlie, and win away.[8] Assure thyselff, man, thow sall find it sa." Mr Piter lauches, and sayes he was worthe the wyne, whow ever it was ; for the twa men war verie read and tead-lyk faced, for ploukes [9] and lumpes. And in deid it cam sa to pass, for they brought hame a notable decreit of reduction of a few of the Freires-yeard against Jhone Grame ; and the uther, by moyen and ernest solistation, gat the action delayit, and brought to arbitriment.

[1] unlucky.　　　　[2] anxious.　　　　[3] table.　　　　[4] cup.
[5] a red-headed toad leap out of it.
[6] red-nosed.　　　　　　　　　[7] treasurers.
[8] by some wile shall presently avoid the issue and escape.
[9] pimples.

THE GENERAL ASSEMBLIES AND THE
EDINBURGH MINISTERS

It was a maist pleasand and confortable thing to be
present at these Assemblies,[1] thair was sic frequencie
and reverence ; with halines in zeall at the doctrine
quhilk soundit mightelie, and the Sessiones at everie
meiting, whar, efter ernest prayer, maters war gravlie
and cleirlie proponit ; overtures maid be the wysest ;
douttes reasonit and discussit be the lernedest and maist
quik ; and, finalie, all withe a voice concluding upon
maters resolved and cleirit, and referring things intricat
and uncleired to farder advysment. Namlie, it is to be
noted, that in all these Assemblies anent the Polecie,[2]
ther was nocht sic a thing as a careing away of anie
poinct with a number of vottes, an or ma, or by a pre-
occupied purpose or led course ; bot maters indifferentlie
proponit, and efter beging light of God, and sersing the
Scripture by conference and reasoning discussit,[3] with
large and sufficient tyme takin and diligentlie employed
for that effect, all with a voice, in an consent and unitie
of mynd, determines and concludes.

God glorified him self notablie with that ministerie
of Edinbruche, in these dayes. The men haid knawlage,
uprightnes, and zeall ; they dwelt verie commodiuslie
togidder, as in a Collage, with a wounderfull consent in
varietie of giftes, all strak on a string and soundet a
harmonie. Jhone Dury[4] was of small literature, bot

---

[1] The General Assemblies of the Church of Scotland which were held
in Edinburgh in 1578 and 1579 and in Stirling in 1578.

[2] The Policy of the Church of Scotland, especially with regard to
bishops.

[3] It was then sometimes the custom of the General Assembly to refer
a matter of controversy to a small committee. Some members of the
committee were specifically appointed to argue in favour of the proposal,
the others to argue against it. After debate, the committee reported its
decision to the Assembly which accepted it without further discussion.

[4] John Durie (1537-1600), James Melville's father-in-law, became
minister of St Giles in 1573, was banished from Edinburgh in 1582, and
sent into ward at Montrose in 1583. Shortly afterwards he became
minister of Montrose.

haid sein and marked the grait warks of God in the first Reformation, and bein a doer bathe with toung and hand. He haid bein a diligent heirar of Mr Knox, and observer of all his wayes. He conceavit the best grounds of maters weill, and could utter tham fearlie, fullie, and fecfullie,[1] with a mightie spreit, voice, and action. The speciall gift I marked in him was halines, and a daylie [and nightlie] cearfull, continuall walking with God in meditation and prayer. He was a verie guid fallow, and tuk delyt, as his speciall comfort, to haiff his table and houss filled with the best men. These he wald gladlie heir, with tham confer and talk, professing he was bot a buik-bearer, and wald fean lern of thame ; and getting the ground and light of knawlage in anie guid poinct, then wald he rejoyse in God, praise and pray thairupon, and urge it with sa cleir and forcible exhortation in Assemblies and pulpit, that he was estimed a verie fordersum[2] instrument. Ther ludgit in his house at all these Assemblies in Edinbruche, [for comoun,] Mr Andro Melvill, Mr Thomas Smeton,[3] Mr Alexander Arbuthnot,[4] thrie of the lernedest in Europe ; Mr James Melvill, my uncle,[5] Mr James Balfour,[6] David Fergusone,[7] David Home,[8] ministers ; with sum zelus, godlie barrones and gentilmen. In tyme of mealles was reasoning upon guid purposes, namlie, maters in hand ; thairefter ernest and lang prayer ; thairefter a chaptour read, and everic man about gaiff his not and observation thairof : Sa that giff all haid bein sett down in wryt, I haiff hard the lernedest and of best judgment say, they wald nocht haiff wissed a fuller and better commentar nor[9] sum tymes wald fall out in that exerceise. Thairefter

---

[1] capably. [2] progressive, helpful. [3] See p. 34.
[4] Alexander Arbuthnot (1538-1583), Principal of King's College, Aberdeen, 1569 ; minister of Old Machar, 1574.
[5] See p. 18. [6] See p. 18.
[7] David Fergusson (d. 1598), minister of Dunfermline, 1560-1598 ; compiled a collection of Scottish proverbs.
[8] David Home (d. c. 1600), minister of Oldhamstocks, 1569 ; translated to Coldingham, 1584.
[9] than.

was sung a Psalme ; efter the quhilk was conference
and deliberation upon the purposes in hand ; and at
night, befor going to bed, ernest and zealus prayer,
according to the esteat and success of maters. And
often tymes, yea, almost daylie, all the Collage was
togidder in an or uther of thair housses ; for, befor
Mr James Lawsone [1] and Mr Walter [2] war maried, they
war burdit with Jhone Durie, and efter entring to thair
awin housses, keipit exceiding guid fallowschipe togidder.

PURPOSE OF MARRIAGE

Heir I man remember a singular benefit of God's
providence and government towards me. I was then
in the floure of my age, about a twa and twentie and
thrie and twentie yeirs ; a young man nocht unlovlie,
and of nature verie loving and amorus, quhilk was the
proped [3] schot of Sathan wharby to snare me, and spoill
the haill wark of God in me. Manie lovers haid I,
and sum loves also ; monie occasiones, in dyvers places
and sortes of persones, and nocht of inferior rank : Yit
my guid God, of his frie grace and love towards me, a
vean, vyll, corrupt youthe ; partlie by his fear wrought
in my heart, partlie by necessar occupation in my calling,
and partlie be a certean schamfastnes of a bashfull nature,
quilk he pat in me, sa keipit me that I was nocht overcome
nor miscaried be na woman, offensivlie to his Kirk, nor
greivuslie to my conscience, in blotting of my bodie. I
markit befor the occasion I haid of lerning to sing and
play on instruments of music in St Androis, wharof my
hart was verie desirus, [bot from grait skill, wherin God
keipit me ;] far graitter and sweittar haid I in Glasgw
of a gentilman's houss in the town, wha interteined maist
expert singars and playars, and brought upe all his

---

[1] See p. 34.
[2] Walter Balcanquhal (1548-1617), admitted to St Giles, 1574;
translated to Trinity Church, 1598.
[3] appointed, deliberate.

berns thairin, namlie, his eldest douchtar, a verie pleasand gentilwoman, endewit with manie guid verteus. I haid everie yeir sum of this gentilman's sonnes my schollars, and be that occasion was hamlie in his houss, and maist lovinglie and hartlie interteined. Affection enterit verie extreamlie betwix that gentlewoman and me, bot as God and man bathe knew, honest and cheast; [1] yit sic as giff my God, and the cairfull and fatherlie admonitiones and conforts of my uncle, haid nocht supplied, it haid undone me. Manie sear [2] battels and greivus tenta-tiounes [3] did my God uphauld me in, and carie me throw; and at last put in my hart a purpose to seik and use that holie and lawfull remeid of mariage; and thairin, namlie to respect a helpe and confort for that calling wherunto I haid advowit my selff. Sa, be my hanting [4] to the Generall Assemblies in Edinbruche, and takin with the godlie ordour and excerceise in the familie of Jhone Durie, and with that cairfull walkine with God I saw in him; as also with sum appeirance of God's fear and honestie I saw in the face and fasones [5] of the bern, being bot about alleavin or twall yeirs of age, I resolvit with my God to settle my hart ther, tak hir for my love, and put all uther out of my hart : And this almost a four yeir befor our mariage.

JAMES VI AND HIS ADVISERS

At that tyme it was a pitie to sie sa weill a brought upe Prince till his bernhead was past, to be sa miserablie corrupted in the entress of his springall [6] age, bathe with sinistrus and fals information of all proceidings in his minoritie, and with evill and maist dangerus grundes and principalles in government of Kirk and Comoun-weill. Then was he maid to think warst of the best men that ever servit in this Kirk and Countrey; to think the haill maner of Reformation of Religion to

[1] chaste.	[2] sore.	[3] temptations.
[4] resorting.	[5] fashions, *i.e.* conduct.	[6] stripling.

haiff bein done be a privie faction, turbulentlie and treasonablie ; to suspect the noble men and haill ministerie that stude for the cause of Religion and his croun against his mother's faction ; yea, to tak course against them, and put at tham as his unfrinds.[1] Amangs the rest, Captan James [2] put the opinion of absolut powar in his Majestie's head ; . . . Sic lyk Mr Patrik Adamsone, Bischope of St Androis,[3] a grait counsellour in these dayes, amangs manie uther evill grounds wharof we will heir heirefter, inculcat this : " That a Christian King sould be the cheif governour of the Kirk, and behovit to have Bischops under him, to hald all in order, conform to antiquite and maist flurissing esteat of the Christian Kirk under the best Emperour, Constantine. And that the discipline of the Kirk of Scotland could nocht stand with a frie kingdome and monarchie, sic as was his Majestie's in Scotland," &c.

A VISIT TO GEORGE BUCHANAN

That September, in tyme of vacans, my uncle, Mr Andro, Mr Thomas Buchanan,[4] and I, heiring that Mr George Buchanan was weak, and his Historie under the press, past ower to Edinbruche annes earend,[5] to visit him and sie the wark. When we cam to his chalmer, we fand him sitting in his chaire, teatching his young

[1] enemies.

[2] Captain James Stewart (d. 1596), granted Earldom of Arran ; obtained great influence over King James after 1583 ; Chancellor of Scotland, 1584 ; lost favour and banished, 1586 ; returned as Captain James Stewart, but failed to regain his position at court ; murdered, 1596.

[3] Patrick Adamson (1537-1592) ; held various charges after the Reformation ; became Archbishop of St Andrews, 1576 ; ambassador to England, 1583 ; uncompromising opponent of Presbyterianism ; excommunicated by Synod of Fife, 1583, but sentence annulled ; excommunicated by General Assembly, 1588. (See also p. 32.)

[4] Thomas Buchanan (c. 1520-1599), Regent in St Salvator's College ; joint Rector of Edinburgh High School, 1568 ; Rector of Stirling Grammar School, 1571 ; minister of Ceres, 1578. He was a nephew of George Buchanan.

[5] on set purpose.

man that servit him in his chalmer to spell a, b, ab ;
e, b, eb, &c. Efter salutation, Mr Andro sayes, " I sie,
Sir, yie are nocht ydle." " Better this," quoth he, " nor
stelling sheipe, or sitting ydle, quhilk is als ill ! " Thairefter he schew us the Epistle Dedicatorie to the King ;
the quhilk, when Mr Andro haid read, he tauld him
that it was obscure in sum places, and wanted certean
words to perfyt the sentence. Sayes he, " I may do na
mair, for thinking on another mater." " What is that ? "
sayes Mr Andro. " To die ! " quoth he ; " bot I leave
that and manie ma things for yow to helpe." [He was
telling him also of Blakwod's [1] answer to his buik, *De Jure
Regni*.]

We went from him to the printar's wark-hous, whom
we fand at the end of the 17 Buik of his Cornicle, at a
place quhilk we thought verie hard for the tyme, quhilk
might be an occasion of steying [2] the haill wark, anent
the buriall of Davie.[3] Thairfor, steying the printer from
proceiding, we cam to Mr George again, and fund him
bedfast by [4] his custome ; and asking him, whow he did ?
" Even going the way of weilfare," sayes he. Mr Thomas,
his cusing, schawes him of the hardnes of that part of
his Storie, that the King wald be offendit with it, and
it might stey all the wark. " Tell me, man," sayes he,
" giff I have tauld the treuthe ? " " Yis," sayes Mr
Thomas, " Sir, I think sa." " I will byd his fead,[5] and
all his kin's, then ! " quod he : " Pray, pray to God for
me, and let Him direct all ! " Sa, be [6] the printing of
his Cornicle was endit, that maist lerned, wyse, and
godlie man, endit this mortall lyff.

" OUR COMMISSION SALBE DISCHARGIT "

To that Convention [7] cam the Erle of Hountlie, weill
accompanied with his frinds, in whase favours, to the

---

[1] Adam Blackwood (1539-1613), educated at and taught philosophy
in the University of Paris ; engaged in controversy with Buchanan.
[2] stopping.   [3] Rizzio.   [4] contrary to.
[5] feud.   [6] by the time that.   [7] Held at Perth in 1582.

grait hurt of the Forbasses, the King gaiff out a decreit-arbitrall.[1] Newes war sparpelit athort[2] the countrey, that the Ministers war all to be thair massacred ; quhilk moved me go repear[3] to Perthe with diligence, to tak part with my uncle and father in Chryst. Coming ther, Sir James Melvill of Hahill[4] schawes me whow evill my uncle and I was thought of at Court, because of our sermonts in St Androis the tyme of the fast,[5] and our doings and sayings at Assemblies, and counsallit us to depart af the town ; quhilk I schew Mr Andro, and willit sa to do, bot in vean : " For I thank God," sayes he, " I am nocht fleyed[6] nor feible-spirited in the cause and message of Chryst. Com what God pleases to send, our commission salbe dischargit ! "

At last the Commissionars of the Kirk war callit, wha, coming in befor the King and his Counsall, delyverit thair Greiffes and Articles[7] ; quhilk being read, Captan James[8] beginnes to threttin, with thrawin[9] brow, and bosting[10] langage. "What ! " sayes he, " wha dar subscryve thir treasonable Articles ? " &c. Mr Andro answeres, " We dar, and wil subscryve tham, and gif our lyves in the cause ! " And withc all starts to, and taks the pen fra the Clark, and subscryves, and calles to the rest of the breithring with couragius speitches ; wha all cam and subscryvit. This bauldnes, when the

---

[1] In 1581 and 1582 some Jesuit priests sent by the Pope and by the King of Spain were in Scotland. It was known that they had had dealings with various Roman Catholic nobles, including the Duke of Lennox and the Earl of Huntly, and suspected that James himself had been in touch with them. James's attitude to Huntly seemed to confirm this suspicion. A " decreit-arbitrall " was the decree, or finding, of an arbiter.

[2] spread throughout. [3] repair.

[4] Sir James Melville of Halhill (1535-1617), courtier and diplomat ; his autobiography is a valuable source-book.

[5] The General Assembly which met at St Andrews in April 1582, appointed a general fast to be kept in June, " the causses wharof was conspiracie of Papists, oppression and thraldom of the Kirk, etc."

[6] afraid.

[7] By command of the King, the General Assembly had drawn up a list of thirteen " Greiffes (i.e. grievances) of the Kirk."

[8] See p. 47. [9] knitted.

[10] threatening.

D

Duc [1] and Captan perceavit, they gatherit thairon that
the Kirk haid a bak,[2] and becam effrayit ; and efter
sum calmer langage, dimissit tham in peace, whom
everie an supposed they sould haiff bein hardliar delt
withall.

MR ANDREW OBEYS A SUMMONS

Whill he [3] is a bissie Bischope about thir things in
outting,[4] as the cours was layed, they war nocht ydle at
hame ; for, in the beginning of Februar, Mr Andro
Melvin is summoned to compeir befor the King and
Counsall within les nor thrie dayes,[5] to answer to sic
things as war to be leyit to his charge, anent certean
speitches uttered be him from pulpit, seditius and
treasonable. Mr Andro compeircd, accompanied with
sum of his schollars and frinds, amangs whom was
Mr Robert Bruce [6] ; and I being in Angus, convoying
my mother-in-law to hir housband, gon away a day
befor his summonding, maid diligence, and cam to
Edinbruche the day of his second compeirance. The
quhilk day he declyned the judicator of the King and
Counsall, being accusit upon na civill cryme or trans-
gression, but upon his doctrin uttered from pulpit. The
quhilk, when the King and Captan James, then maid
Grait Chancellar, with roarings of lyones and mcssages
of dcathe, haid taken sa hat, that all the Counsell and
Courtes of the Palice war filled with fear, noyes, and

---

[1] Lennox. Esmé Stuart (1542 ?-1583), first Duke of Lennox, came to
Scotland in 1579 as agent of the Guises ; pretended to embrace Protestant-
ism but had to leave Scotland in 1582.

[2] backing.

[3] Patrick Adamson, Archbishop of St Andrews (see p. 32).

[4] in outting = abroad. Adamson went to England at the beginning
of 1584 " to practise the alteration of the haill esteat and discipline of the
Kirk."

[5] " Summoned on Setterday, to compeir on Mounday nixt." Margin
of MS.

[6] Robert Bruce (1554-1631), minister of St Giles, 1587 ; ordered to
leave Edinburgh, 1600.

bruttes,[1] Mr Andro never jarging [2] nor daschit [3] a whit,
withe magnanimus courage, mightie force of sprit, and
fouthe [4] of evidence of reasone and langage, planlie
tauld the King and Counsall, that they presumed ower
bauldlie in a constitut esteat of a Christian Kirk, the
kingdome of Jesus Chryst, passing by and disdeaning the
prophets, pastors, and doctors of the Kirk, to tak upon
tham to judge the doctrin, and controll the ambassators
and messingers of a King and Counsall graitter nor
they, and far above tham !   " And that," sayes he, " yie
may sie your weaknes, owersight, and rashnes, in takin
upon yow that quhilk yie nather aught nor can do,"
(lowsing a litle Hebrew Byble fra his belt, and clanking
it down on the burd befor the King and Chancelar,)
" Thair is," says he, " my instructiones and warrand ;
let sie quhilk of yow can judge thairon, or controll me
thairin, that I haiff past my injunctiones ! "   The
Chanclar, opening the buik, findes it Hebrew, and putes
it in the King's hand, saying, " Sir, he skornes your
Majestie and Counsall."   " Na, my lord," sayes Mr
Andro, " I skorn nocht ; bot with all ernestnes, zeall,
and gravitie, I stand for the cause of Jesus Chryst and
his Kirk."

INTERLUDE AT SEA

My cusing, being a mariner, conducit a bott to carie
a town of his portage wyn about to Carell,[5] and decking
me upe in his sie attyre betymes in the morning, about
the simmer solstice, tuk me in down under Dondie as a
shipbroken sie-man [6] ; and rowing about, behoved to
go to the heavin of St Androis, to lose a certean of skleatt
steanes [7] ; and because it was law water, we behoved
to ly a whyll in the road till the water grew, whare the

---

[1] rumours.   [2] flinching.   [3] dismayed.
[4] abundance.   [5] Crail.
[6] Melville was in danger of arrest as a result of the situation created
by the passing of the Black Acts in May 1584 (see Introduction, p. 11).
[7] to unload a consignment of slates.

bott wanting ane owerlaft,[1] the seall was cassen ower hir ta end,[2] and ther I leyed upe, lest I sould be spyed of sum shipes rydding besyde. Bot within schort space, partlie be rokking in the sie, and partlie for want of eare,[3] I grew sa extream seik, that manie a tyme I besaught my cowsing to sett me a-land ; schosin rather anie sort of dethe, for a guid cause, nor sa to be tormented in a stinking holl. And yit, whowbeit it was extream peanfull, I gatt ther notable medicin of vomitine, quhilk was a preservative to my helthe all that yeir.

MR ANDREW TEACHES THE KING AND CONFOUNDS THE ARCHBISHOP

About the end of Junie,[4] his Majestie cam to St Androis, and brought with him the said Du Bartas,[5] and coming first without anie warning to the New Collage, he calles for Mr Andro, saying he was com with that gentleman to haiff a Lessone. Mr Andro answeres, That he haid teatched his ordinar that day in the fornoone. " That is all ane," sayes the King, " I mon haiff[6] a lessone, and be heir within an houre for that effect." And, indeid, within les nor an houre, his Majestie was in the scholl, and the haill Universitie convenit with him ; befor whom Mr Andro *ex tempore* intreated maist cleirlie and mightelie of the right government of Chryst, and in effect refuted the haill Actes of Parliament maid against the discipline thairof, to the grait instruction and confort of his auditor, except the King allean, wha was verie angrie all that night.

Upon the morn the Bischope[7] haid bathe a prepared

---

[1] *i.e.* it was an open boat with no deck (loft).
[2] the sail was cast over one end of her.
[3] air.
[4] 1587.
[5] Guillaume de Salluste du Bartas, a poet of European renown, came to Scotland in 1587 on a secret mission concerning a proposal that James VI should marry the Princess of Navarre.
[6] must have.   [7] Patrick Adamson (see p. 47).

lessone and feast maid for the King. His lessone was a
tichted upe abregment [1] of all he haid tetched [2] the yeir
bypast, namlie, anent the corrupt groundes quhilk he
haid put in the King's head, contrarie to the trew discipline. To the quhilk lessone Mr Andro went, contrar
to his custome, and withe his awin pen market all his
fals grounds and reasones, and, without farder, caussit
ring his bell at twa efternoone the sam day ; wharof
the King heiring, he send to Mr Andro, desyring him to
be moderat, and haiff regard to his presence, utherwayes
he wald discharge him. He answered couragiouslie,
that his Majestie's ear and tender breist was pitifullie
and dangeruslie filled with errours and untreuthes be
that wicked man, the quhilk he could nocht suffer to
pas, and bruik a lyff, utherwayes, except the stopping
of the breathe of God's mouthe, and prejudging of his
treuthe, he sould behaiff him selff maist moderatlie and
reverentlie to his Majestie, in all respects. The King
send againe to him and me, desyring it sould be sa, and
schawin that he wald haiff his four hours [3] in the Collage,
and drink with Mr Andro. Sa coming to that lessone
with the Bischope, wha requysted the King for leive to
mak answer instantlie, in cais anie thing war spoken
against his doctrine. Bot ther Mr Andro, making him
as thouche he haid na thing to do but with the Papist,
brings out thair works, and reids out of tham all the
Bischopes grounds and reasones. The quhilk, when he
haid at lainthe and maist cleirlie schawin to be plean
Papistrie, then he settes against the sam with all his
mean, [4] and with invincible force of reasone, from cleir
grounds of Scripture, with a mightie parrhesie [5] and
fluide of eloquence, he dinges tham sa down, that the
Bischope was dasht and strukken als dum as the stok [6]
he satt upon ! Efter the lessone, the King, in his mother

---

[1] a close summary (tightened-up abridgment).
[2] taught.   [3] his four o'clock repast.   [4] might.
[5] parrhesia or frankness of speech.
[6] block of wood ; probably here a wooden chair.

toung, maid sum distingoes,[1] and discoursit a whyll
thairon, and gaiff certean injunctiones to the Universitie
for reverencing and obeying of his Bischope ; wha, fra
that day furthe, began to tyre of his teatching, and fall
mair and mair in disgrace and confusion. The King,
with Monsieur du Bartas, cam to the Collage Hall, wher
I causit prepear, and haiff in readines a banquet of wat
and dry confectiones, with all sortes of wyne, wharat
his Majestie camped [2] verie mirrelie a guid whyll, and
thairefter went to his hors. Bot Monsieur du Bartas
taried behind and conferrit with my uncle and me a
wholl houre, and syne followed efter the King ; wha
inquyring of him that night, as ane tauld me, " What
was his judgment of the twa he haid herd in St Androis ? "
He answeret the King, " That they war bathe lerned
men, bot the Bischope's war cunned,[3] and prepared
maters, and Mr Andro haid a grait reddie store of all
kynd of lerning within him ; and by [4] that, Mr Andro
his spreit and courage was far above the other." The
quhilk judgment the King approved.

A SHIP OF THE SPANISH ARMADA COMES TO ANSTRUTHER

That wintar [5] the King was occupied in commenting
of the Apocalypse, and in setting out of sermontes
thairupon against the Papists and Spainyarts : And yit,
by a piece of grait owersight, the Papists practeised
never mair bisselie in this land, and maid graitter
preparation for receaving of the Spainyarts nor [6] that
yeir. For a lang tyme the ncwes of a Spanishe navie
and armie haid bein blasit abrode ; and about the
Lambes tyde of the 1558, this Yland haid fund a feirfull
effect thairof, to the utter subversion bathe of Kirk and
Polecie, giff God haid nocht wounderfullie watched
ower the sam, and mightelie fauchten and defeat that

---

[1] distinctions.   [2] diverted himself.
[3] learned by heart, prepared beforehand.   [4] besides.
[5] 1587-1588.   [6] than.

armie be his souldiours, the elements, quhilk he maid
all four maist fercelie to afflict tham till almost utter
consumption. Terrible was the feir, persing war the
pretchings,[1] ernest, zealus, and fervent war the prayers,
sounding war the siches [2] and sobbes, and abounding
was the teares at that Fast and Generall Assemblie
keipit at Edinbruche,[3] when the newes war crediblie
tauld, sum tymes of thair landing at Dumbar, sum tymes
at St Androis, and in Tay, and now and then at Aberdein
and Cromertie first : And in verie deid, as we knew
certeanlie soone efter, the Lord of Armies, wha ryddes
upon the winges of the wounds,[4] the Keipar of his awin
Israell, was in the mean tyme convoying that monstruus
navie about our costes, and directing thair hulkes and
galiates to the ylands, rokkes, and sandes, wharupon he
haid destinat thair wrak and destruction. For within
twa or thrie monethe thairefter, earlie in the morning,
be brak of day, ane of our bailyies cam to my bedsyde,[5]
saying, (but nocht with fray [6]) " I haiff to tell yow
newes, Sir. Ther is arryvit within our herbrie this
morning a schipe full of Spainyarts, bot nocht to giff
mercie bot to ask ! " And sa schawes me that the
Commanders haid landit, and he haid commandit tham
to thair schipe againe till the Magistrates of the town
haid advysit, and the Spainyarts haid humblie obeyit :
Therfor desyrit me to ryse and heir thair petition with
tham. Upe I got with diligence, and assembling the
honest men of the town, cam to the Tolbuthe ; and
efter consultation taken to heir tham, and what answer
to mak, ther presentes us a verie reverend man of big
stature, and grave and stout countenance, grey-heared,
and verie humble lyk, wha, efter mikle and verie law
courtessie, bowing down with his face neir the ground,
and twitching my scho [7] with his hand, began his harang
in the Spanise toung, wharof I understud the substance ;

---

[1] piercing were the preachings.   [2] sighs.
[3] This Assembly was held in February 1588.   [4] winds.
[5] at Anstruther.   [6] fear.   [7] touching my shoe.

and being about to answer in Latine, he haiffing onlie a young man with him to be his interpreter, began and tauld ower againe to us in guid Einglis. The sum was, that King Philipe, his maister, haid riget out a navie and armie to land in Eingland for just causes to be advengit of manie intolerable wrangs quhilk he haid receavit of that nation ; but God for ther sinnes haid bein against thame, and be storme of wather haid dryven the navie by the cost [1] of Eingland, and him with a certean of Capteanes, being the Generall of twentie hulks, upon an yll of Scotland, called the Fear Yll,[2] wher they maid schipewrak, and whar sa monie as haid eschapit the merciles sies and rokes, haid mair nor sax or sevin ouks suffred grait hunger and cauld, till conducing that bark out of Orkney, they war com hither as to thair speciall frinds and confederats to kiss the King's Majestie's hands of Scotland, (and thairwith bekkit evcn to the yeard,[3]) and to find releiff and comfort thairby to him selff, these gentilmen Capteanes, and the poore souldarts, whase condition was for the present maist miserable and pitifull.

I answerit this mikle, in soum [4] : That whowbeit nather our frindschipe, quhilk could nocht be grait, seing ther King and they war frinds to the graitest enemie of Chryst, the Pape of Rome, and our King and we defyed him, nor yit thair cause against our nibours and speciall frinds of Eingland could procure anie benefit at our hands for thair releiff and confort ; nevertheles, they sould knaw be experience, that we war men, and sa moved be human compassione, and Christiannes of better relligion nor they, quhilk sould kythe,[5] in the fruicts and effect, plan contrar to thars. For wheras our peiple resorting amangs tham in peacable and lawfull effeares of merchandise, war violentlie takin

---

[1] past the coast.
[2] Fair Isle, midway between the Orkneys and the Shetlands.
[3] bowed, even to the earth.
[4] in brief.
[5] appear.

and cast in prisone, thair guids and gear confiscat, and thair bodies committed to the crewall flaming fyre for the cause of Relligion, they sould find na thing amangs us bot Christian pitie and warks of mercie and almes, leaving to God to work in thair harts concerning Relligion as it pleased him. This being trewlie reported again to him be his trunshman,[1] with grait reverence he gaiff thankes, and said he could nocht mak answer for thair Kirk and the lawes and ordour thairof, onlie for him selff, that ther war divers Scotsmen wha knew him, and to whome he haid schawin courtesie and favour at Calles,[2] and as he supposit, sum of this sam town of Anstruther. Sa schew him that the Bailyies granted him licence with the Capteanes, to go to thair ludging for thair refreschment, bot to nane of thair men to land, till the ower-lord of the town[3] war advertised, and understand the King's Majestie's mynd anent thame. Thus with grait courtessie he departed.

That night, the Lard[4] being advertised, cam, and on the morn, accompanied with a guid nomber of the gentilmen of the countrey round about, gaiff the said Generall and the Capteanes presence, and efter the sam speitches, in effect, as befor, receavit tham in his hous, and interteined tham humeanlie, and sufferit the souldiours to com a-land, and ly all togidder, to the number of threttin score, for the maist part young berdles men, sillie, trauchled, and houngered,[5] to the quhilk a day or twa, keall,[6] pattage,[7] and fische was giffen ; for my advyse was conforme to the Prophet Elizeus his to the King of Israel, in Samaria, " Giff tham bread and water," &c. The names of the commanders war Jan Gomes de Medina, Generall of twentie houlkes, Capitan Patricio, Capitan de Legoretto, Capitan de Luffera, Capitan Mauritio, and Seingour Serrano.

---

[1] interpreter (Fr. *trucheman*).   [2] Calais.
[3] overlord of the town, *i.e.* the Laird of Anstruther.
[4] laird.   [5] feeble, bedraggled, and hungry.
[6] kail.   [7] broth (Fr. *potage*).

Bot verelie all the whyll my hart melted within me for desyre of thankfulnes to God, when I rememberit the prydfull and crewall naturall of they [1] peiple, and whow they wald haiff usit us in ceas they haid landit with thair forces amangs us ; and saw the wounderfull wark of God's mercie and justice in making us sie tham, the cheiff commanders of tham to mak sic dewgard [2] and curtessie to pure simen, [3] and thair souldarts [4] so abjectlie to beg almes at our dures [5] and in our streites.

In the mean tyme, they knew nocht of the wrak of the rest, but supposed that the rest of the armie was saifflie returned, till a day I gat in St Androis in print the wrak of the Galliates in particular, with the names of the principall men, and whow they war usit in Yrland and our Hilands, in Walles, and uther partes of Eingland ; the quhilk when I recordit to Jan Gomes, be particular and speciall names, O then he cryed out for greiff, bursted and grat. This Jan Gomes schew grait kyndnes to a schipe of our town, quhilk he fund arrested at Calles at his ham-coming, red [6] to court for hir, and maid grait rus [7] of Scotland to his King, tuk the honest men to his hous, and inquyrit for the Lard of Anstruther, for the Minister, and his host, and send hame manie commendationes. Bot we thanked God with our hartes, that we haid sein tham amangs us in that forme.

MR ANDREW MAKES AN OFFER

My uncle, Mr Andro, using alwayes to speak planlie, with zeall and birning affectiones to the honour of God and the King's weill, gaiff him at this time [8] a maist scharpe and frie admonition concerning his evill thinking and speaking of the best frinds of Chryst and him selff,

---

[1] these.   [2] salutation (Fr. *Dieu garde*).
[3] poor seamen.   [4] soldiers.   [5] doors.
[6] rode.   [7] praise.
[8] This appears under date 1593. After the affair of the Spanish Blanks, the Kirk thought that the King was showing too much clemency to the Roman Catholic nobles (including Huntly).

the Guid Regent,[1] Mr Knox, and Mr George Bowchanan ;
and his thinking weill and favouring of Chryst and his
graitest enemies the Papists, and, namlie, that Hous of
Hountlie ; desyring, confidentlie, that sic as war his
counsallours thairin sould kythe in presence of the
Esteatts, and giff he convicted tham nocht of fals, treasonable, and maist pernitius doing thairin against Chryst,
the King's persone, his esteat and realme, he sould nocht
refuse to go to the gibbet for it, provyding they being
convict sould ga the sam gett ! [2] Withe the quhilk the
King and his Counsellors comported, and past ower
the mater with smylling, saying the man was mair
zealus and coleric nor wyse.

MR JAMES'S WAY WITH THE KING

Thairefter [3] a Commission, with the sentence pro-
nuncit be the Synod of Fyff against the rest,[4] was approven
and ratefied be the haill Assemblie, acknawlaging thairin
the speciall benefeit of God's providence in steiring upe
the spreits of his servants to be wacryff,[5] cearfull, and
curagius in the wark of his glorie and cause of his Kirk.
And during the tyme of Assemblie was directed, with
Commissionars, certean Articles and Petitiones to the
King. Amangs the quhilk commissionars I being named,
sum said it was nocht convenient, being suspected and
evill-lyked of be the King. To the quhilk opinion the
Assemblie beginning to inclyne, I stud upe and said
" I haid bein employed in commission oft tymes against
my will, and when things was mair peanfull and dangerus,
even when uthers refusit ; bot now, even for the reasone
quhilk was alleagit, I wald requeist for it as a benefit

[1] Moray (see p. 22).
[2] should go the same way.
[3] This refers to the General Assembly in May 1594.
[4] In October 1593 the Synod of Fife excommunicated six of the
leading " Papist Erles and Lords." One of them, Lord Home, received
absolution from the General Assembly in May 1594 ; the sentence against
the others was confirmed.   [5] watchful.

of the breithring to send me, quhilk wald be the onlie way to cleir bathe them and mie of suspition and sklander, for even utherwayes I meined to present my selff at Court befor the King, to sie gif anie man haid ought to say to me." Of this the breithring war glaid, and resolved, in a voice,[1] to send me. Sa, coming to Sterling, whar the King was, far by [2] our expectatioun we war maist gratiouslie accepted.

All our Articles war reasonit and answerit be his Majestie's awin hand-wryt upon the mergent,[3] and that verie favourablie, to our grait contentment ; and thairefter, I, that was the grait tratour, with the rest callit in to the Cabbinet with the King allean ! His Majestie beginnes to regrat that he could nocht find that freindlines in the Kirk quhilk he cravit and wissed.[4] I, haiffing the speitche, answered, Ther was a peccant humor in the body quhilk behovcd to be purged, or it could nocht be out of danger of disease, yea, deathe. The King asked me what that was ? I said it was sus-pition on ather syde ; for purging wharof it war best we sould be frie on ather syde, and schaw our greiffs and occasiones of suspecting the warst, the quhilk being removit, the body wald be curit and haill. The King thought it maist meit and pertinent, and begins and expones what he haid [to say ?].

First, concerning the assembling of his subjects without his licence :—To the quhilk we answerit, we did it be the warrant of his Majestie's lawes, and of Chryst according to the Word, and custom of our Kirk sen the beginning ; quhilk nather haid, nor be God's grace ever sould be to his Majestie's hurt, bot honour and weill.

Second, concerning the excommunicating of his speciall servant and noble-man, the Lord Home :—We answerit, That he was a profest dangerus Papist, in course with the rest, and whowsone he repented and

[1] unanimously.　　　　[2] beyond.
[3] margin.　　　　[4] wished.

reteired from them, as we war in guid hope he sould do, and approve him selff to the present Assemblie, he sould be relaxed, and his Majestie satisfeit thairanent.

The Third and last was concerning Mr Andro Hountar, Minister,[1] wha haid kythed [2] in open fields with Bodwell [3] :—We answerit, that incontinent thairefter the Presbyterie of St Androis haid proceidit against him, and haid deposit him of his office of Ministerie.

Then his Majestie ceassing, I asked, if his Majestie haid anie thing to say to me? He answerit, Na thing mair nor to all the rest, saiff that he saw me ane in all commissiones! I answerit, I thanked God thairfor, for thairin I was serving God, his Kirk, and the King publictlie, and as for anie privat unlawfull or undewtifull practise, I wald wis traducars (if anie was of me to his Majestie) sould be maid to schaw thair face befor ther King, as I presentlie haid procured of the Kirk to do, of sett purpose. And thairefter exponing all our greiffs and petitiones, receavit, as said is, verie guid answers, namlie a promise of a Parliament with all convenient diligence, wharin these excommunicat Papist Erles sould be forefaultit,[4] and thairefter proceidit against with fyre and sword. Efter the quhilk, the King, taking me asyde, caussit ushe [5] the Cabinet, and ther conferrit with me at lainthe alean of all purposes, and gaiff me speciall commendationes and directiones to my uncle Mr Andro, whom with me he acknawlagit to be maist fathfull and trustie subjects. Sa of the strang working of God, I, that cam to Sterling the trator, retourned to Edinbruche a grait courteour, yea a Cabinet Counsallour! And sa,

---

[1] Of Newburn in Fifeshire, to which charge he was admitted in 1588. Hunter was deposed by the General Assembly on 17th May 1594, " being bruitit and suspectit to have joynit himselfe with the Kings rebells " (*Booke of the Universall Kirk*, iii, 842). He went to the Low Countries and became chaplain to one of the Scottish regiments there.

[2] appeared.

[3] Francis Stewart Hepburn, fifth Earl of Bothwell (*d.* 1624), who had headed various treasonable risings.

[4] subjected to forfeiture.

[5] dissolved.

indeid, continowed till these Papist Erls war brought
hame and restored againe,[1] as we will heir at lainthe
heirefter.

MR ANDREW'S WAY WITH THE KING

Sa, in the monethe of August 1595, the said Mr David [2]
and my uncle ar chargit to compeir befor the King and
Counsall at Falkland, to answer for certean speitches
uttered be tham in thair doctrin against his Majestie's
progenitours ; of the quhilk I knew na thing bot be
advertisment fra my uncle from St Androis to keipe the
dyet. Coming to Falkland, the King inquyres of me,
What I thought of Mr David Blak? I answerit, " I
thought him a guid and godlie man, and a mightie
preatchour, and a man whase ministerie haid bein verie
forcible and fruitfull in St Androis." —" O ", sayes the
King, " yie ar the first man, and onlie, that ever I hard
speak guid of him amangs ministerie, gentilmen, or
burgesses ! "—" Surlie, then, (says I,) I am verie sorie,
Sir, that your Majestie hes nocht spoken with the best
sort of them all."—" I ken," sayes the King in coler,
" the best, and hes spoken with tham ; bot all your
seditius deallings are cloked, and hes bein with that
name of the best men."—" Then, surlie, (says I,) Sir,
your Majestie sall do weill to giff Mr David a syse [3] of
anie in all tha thrie ranks, excepting nan bot sic as hes
knawin particulars ; and giff they fyle [4] him, I sall
speak na mair in this maner to your Majestie, till your

---

[1] In 1596.

[2] David Black (d. 1603), minister of St Andrews from 1590 to 1597,
incurred the enmity of William Balfour of Burleigh, partly because of his
successful ministry, but mainly because it was proposed to use the house
occupied by Balfour as the parish manse. Balfour (according to James
Melville) carried to the King false and calumnious reports of Black and
of Andrew Melville, his greatest friend. In October 1596 Black preached
a sermon which greatly offended the King and, after a good deal of
bickering, James (in 1597) insisted that he should be translated to Arbirlot
(see p. 12).

[3] assize.   [4] condemn.

Majestie find what he is in effect." The King slipping
away fra me, goes to a speciall courtier, and sayes to him,
" Fathe, Mr James Melvill and I ar at our graittest,[1]
for I perceave he is all for Mr David Blak, and that
sort ! " The King, lest he sould irritat the Kirk be
calling befor his Counsall anie Minister for thair doctrine,
quhilk haid nocht succeidit weill of befor, called onlie
a nomber of the Breithring of the ministerie, (namlie,
sic whilk war offendit with Mr David's scharpe and plean
forme of doctrine, sparing nather King nor Minister,) to
try the mater, and judge thairupon.

Mr David compeiring, declynit the King's judicator,
in doctrine ; and as for the Breithring, he refusit tham
nocht, being anie sort of Assemblie of the Kirk, rightlie
callit for that effect, or utherwayes in privat to confer
with thame, and satisfie tham in anie dout conceavit
of his doctrine. The King summarlie and confusedlie
passit ower all, and put nan of these things to inter-
loquutor, bot called for the witnesses. And Mr David,
called to sie what he haid to say against tham, answerit,
Gif that was a judicator, he sould haiff an answer concerning the unlawfulnes and incompetencie alleagit ; as
lykwayes, put ceas it war,[2] as it is nocht, he sould haiff
an accusar fortifeit with twa witnesses, according to the
rewll of the Apostle, &c. That in lyk maner is past,
and a nomber of witneses is examined, Burley, the
delatter[3] and accusar, being alwayes present : Whilk,
when my uncle, Mr Andro Melvill, perceaving, chapping[4]
at the chalmer dure, whar we war, comes in, and efter
humble reverence done to the King, he braks out with
grait libertie of speitche, letting the King planlie to
knaw, that quhilk dyvers tymes befor with small lyking,[5]
he haid tooned[6] in his ear, " That thair was twa Kings
in Scotland, twa Kingdomes, and twa Jurisdictiones :
Thir was Chryst Jesus, &c. : And gif the King of

---

[1] are on the most friendly terms. [2] if the case were put.
[3] informer. [4] knocking.
[5] with little appreciation. [6] tuned.

Scotland, civill King James the Saxt, haid anie judicator or cause thair, presentlie, it sould nocht be to judge the fathfull messanger of Jesus Chryst, the King, &c., bot (turning him to the Lard of Burley, standing there) this trator, wha hes committed divers poincts of hie treasone against his Majestie's civill lawes, to his grait dishonour and offence of his guid subjects, namlie, taking of his peacable subjects on the night out of thair housses, ravishing of weimen, and receatting [1] within his hous of the King's rebels and forfault enemies ! " &c.

With this, Burley falles down on his knies to the King, and craves justice. " Justice ! " sayes Mr Andro, " wald to God yow haid it ! Yow wald nocht be heir to bring a judgment from Chryst upon the King, and thus falslie and unjustlie to vex and accuse the fathfull servants of God ! " The King began, with sum countenances and speitches, to command silence and dashe him ; bot he, insurging [2] with graitter bauldnes and force of langage, buir [3] out the mater sa, that the King was fean [4] to tak it upe betwix tham with gentill termes and mirrie talk ; saying, " They war bathe litle men, and thair hart was at thair mouthe ! " Sa that meitting was demissit the forenoone. Nather war we assemblit again in anie forme of judicator ; bot, when I perceavit the King to be incensed, and verie evill-myndit bathe against Mr Andro and Mr David, I spak the Erle of Mar, being at Court, informing him of the treuthe of maters, and whow dangerus a thing it was to his Majestie, at sic a tyme, to brak out with the Kirk, whill as Boduell [5] haid confederit [6] with the Papist Lords, and as he knew ther war presentlie a grait commotioun in all the Bordars, besought him thairfor to counsall his Majestie aright, and mitigat these maters. The quhilk he did fathfullie. And sa, the King callit Mr David to him selff, in privat and hamlie maner, desyring to understand the treuthe be way of conference ; the quhilk Mr David schew him

---

[1] harbouring.	[2] overflowing.	[3] bore.
[4] fain.	[5] Bothwell.	[6] allied.

to his satisfactioun. In lyk maner, Mr Andro, wha, efter his fasone, maist frilie reasonit with the King, and tauld him his mynd betwix tham to the King's contentation; and sa, in end, his Majestie directed me, efter lang conference on thir maters, to go to St Androis and teatche, and declar the mater, sa as the peiple might be put out of evill opinion, baithe of his Majestie and thair Minister, and whow that all was weill aggreit.

PLAIN SPEECH FROM MR ANDREW

When the King and Esteattes war sett doun,[1] the King causses the Ministers to be callit upon be nam and lettin in, leaving out Mr Andro, who cam in with the formaist. The King finding fault with him that came ther uncallit, he answers, " Sir, I have a calling to com heir be Chryst Jesus the King, and his Kirk, wha hes speciall entres in this tourn,[2] and against quhilks directlie this Conventioun is mett; charging yow and your Esteattes in his nam, and of his Kirk, that yie favour nocht his enemies whom he hattes, nor go nocht about to call hame and mak citiciners, these that has traterouslie sought to betrey thair citie and native countrey to the crewall Spainyard, with the overthrow of Chryst's Kingdome, fra the quhilk they have bein thairfor maist justlie cutt of as rotten members; certifeing, if they sould do in the contrair, they sould feill the dint of the wrathe of that King and his Esteattes ! " And, braking on in particular upon the graittest part of that Conventioun, with plane speitche and mightie force of zeall, he challengit tham of hiche treasone bathe against Chryst and the King, against the Kirk and countrey of Scotland,

---

[1] In September 1596 the King summoned a Convention of the Estates to Falkland to consider calling home Huntly and Errol, the Roman Catholic lords who had been banished in 1594, though in point of fact Huntly had already returned. To this Convention James summoned, as representatives of the Kirk, a few ministers whom he regarded as compliant. But Andrew Melville, hearing of this and scenting danger, turned up too.

[2] interest in this affair.

in that purpose and counsall they war about. Bot the King interrupted him, and commanded him to go out, whase command he obeyit, thanking God that they haid knawin his mynd, and gottin his message dischargit. Mr David Lindsay,[1] Mr James Nicolson,[2] Mr Patrik Galloway,[3] and I, that remeanit and hard all, and spak in the contrar, adhering in effect to that quhilk Mr Andro haid uttered, bot in sic sort, that the King, with fear promises, satisfeit over easelie and removit. In end, the Esteattes concludes, that the King and Kirk being satisfeit, it war best to call tham hame, and that his Majestie sould heir thair offerres for that effect.

MR ANDREW TALKS THE KING DOWN

Sa, Mrs Andro Melvill, Patrik Galloway, James Nicolsone, and I, cam to Falkland, whar we fand the King verie quyet. The rest leyed [4] upon me to be speaker, alleaging I could propone the mater [5] substantiuslie, and in a myld and smothe maner, quhilk the King lyked best of. And, entering in the Cabinet with the King alan, I schew his Majestie, That the Commissionars of the Generall Assemblie, with certean uther breithring ordeanit to watche for the weill of the Kirk in sa dangerous a tym, haid convenit at Cowper. At the quhilk word the King interrupts me, and crabbotlie [6] quarrels our meitting, alleaging it was without warrand and seditius, making our selves and the countrey

---

[1] David Lindsay (c. 1531-1613), minister of Leith, 1560 ; appointed Bishop of Ross, 1600, holding Leith in conjunction. He was a great favourite with James VI and accompanied him to England in 1603.

[2] James Nicolson (1557-1607), minister of Cortachy, 1580 ; translated to Meigle, 1583 ; Bishop of Dunkeld, 1607.

[3] Patrick Galloway (c. 1551-1627), minister of Fowlis Easter, 1576 ; translated to Perth, 1581 ; fled to England because of suspected Gowrie sympathies ; returned and became domestic chaplain to the King, 1590 ; minister of St Giles, 1607.

[4] laid.

[5] In September 1596 the Commissioners of the General Assembly and certain other ministers met at Coupar and resolved to complain to the King about his lenience to the " Papist Lords."

[6] peevishly.

to conceave feir whar thair was na cause. To the quhilk,
I beginning to reply, in my maner, Mr Andro doucht
nocht [1] abyd it, bot brak af upon the King in sa zealus,
powerfull, and unresistable a maner, that whowbeit the
King used his authoritie in maist crabbit and colerik
maner, yit Mr Andro bure him down, and outtered the
Commission as from the mightie God, calling the King
bot " God's sillie [2] vassall " ; and, taking him be the
sleive, sayes this in effect, throw mikle hat reasoning
and manie interruptiones : " Sir, we will humblie
reverence your Majestie alwayes, namlie in publict, but
sen [3] we have this occasioun to be with your Majestie
in privat, and the treuthe is, yie are brought in extream
danger bathe of your lyff and croun, and with yow the
countrey and Kirk of Christ is lyk to wrak, for nocht
telling yow the treuthe, and giffen of yow a fathfull
counsall, we mon [4] discharge our dewtie thairin, or els
be trators bathe to Christ and yow ! And, thairfor, Sir,
as divers tymes befor, sa now again, I mon tell yow,
thair is twa Kings and twa Kingdomes in Scotland.
Thair is Chryst Jesus the King, and his kingdome the
Kirk, whase subject King James the Saxt is, and of
whase kingdome nocht a king, nor a lord, nor a heid,
bot a member ! And they whome Chryst hes callit
and commandit to watch over his Kirk, and governe
his spirituall kingdome, hes sufficient powar of him, and
authoritie sa to do, bathe togidder and severalie ; the
quhilk na Christian King nor Prince sould controll and
discharge, but fortifie and assist, utherwayes nocht
fathfull subjects nor members of Chryst. And, Sir,
when yie war in your swadling-cloutes, Chryst Jesus
rang [5] friely in this land in spyt of all his enemies, and his
Officers and Ministers convenit and assemblit for the
rewling and weill of his Kirk, quhilk was ever for your
weilfear, defence, and preservatioun also, when thir
sam enemies was seiking your destructioun and cutting
af. And, in sa doing, be thair Assemblies and meittings

[1] could not. [2] simple (*i.e.* of no rank). [3] since. [4] must. [5] reigned.

E 2

sen syne [1] continowalie hes bein terrible to these enemies, and maist stedable [2] for yow. And will yie now, when thair is mair nor extream necessitie of the continowance and fathfull discharge of that dewtie, drawin to your awin destructioun be a devillische and maist pernitius counsall, begin to hinder and dishart [3] Chryst's servants, and your best and maist faithfull subjects, quarrelling tham for thair conveining and cair that they haiff of thair dewtie to Chryst and yow, when yie sould rather commend and countinance tham, as the godlie Kings and guid Emperours did ? As to the wisdome of your counsall, quhilk I call devilishe and pernitius, it is this, that yie mon be servit with all sort of men to come to your purpose and grandour, Jew and Gentill, Papist and Protestant ; and because the Ministers and Protestants in Scotland is over stark,[4] and controlles the King, they mon be waikn[e]d and brought law,[5] be steiring upe a partie to tham, and the King being æquall and indifferent, bathe salbe fean to flie to him ; sa sall he be weill servit. Bot, Sir, gif God's wesdome be the onlie trew wisdome, this will prove mere and mad folie, for his curse can bot light upon it ; sa that, in seiking of bathe, yie sall los bathe, wharas in cleiving uprightlie to God, his trew servants sould be your sure freinds, and he sould compell the rest, counterfitlie and leinglie,[6] to giff over tham selves and serve yow, as he did to David ! "

" THEY HECLED ON "

With this all men of anie mark or valour was practised be Sir Patrik [7] ; and sic as war alreadie woun, and

---

[1] since that time.   [2] serviceable.   [3] dishearten.
[4] too powerful.   [5] low.   [6] lyingly.
[7] This passage refers to the General Assembly held at Dundee in May 1597. Its purpose was to relax the excommunication of the " Papist Lords " and to give assent to certain Articles proposed by the King. Sir Patrick Murray, a gentleman of the bed-chamber (called by Melville " the diligent Apostle of the Northe "), was used by the King to win over, by something akin to bribery, the ministers of the Kirk. " By votting and dealling the King's will was wrought " (*Melville*) " howbeit, a great number of the sincerest sort did their part honestlie " (*Booke of the Universall Kirk*).

brought to be acquented, and to confer with his Majestie. This was the excerceise, morning and evening, diverse dayes. On a night at evin, I, sitting at my supper, Sir Patrik sends for me to confer with him in the kirk-yeard. I, raising from supper, cam to him. The matter was anent my uncle, Mr Andro, whom the King could nocht abyde. I wald do weill to counsall him to return ham, or the King wald discharge him. I answerit, It wald be bot in vean to me sa to do, for he wald nocht tak that counsall; and gif the King wald use his authoritie, he wald suffer patientlie; bot I was certean that deathe wald nocht cause him do against his conscience! "Surlie," sayes he, "I fear he suffer the dint of the King's wrathe!" "And trewlie," said I, "I am nocht fearit bot he will byd all!" Returning to my uncle, whar I left him at supper, I tauld him; whase answer I neid nocht to wrait.

Upon the morn, befor Assemblie tyme, I was commandit to com to the King, and Mr Andro withe me; wha, entering in his Cabbinet, began to dell verie fearlie [1] with my uncle; bot thairefter entering to twitche maters,[2] Mr Andro brak out with his wounted humor of fredome and zeall, and ther they hecled on [3] till all the hous, and clos, bathe hard, mikle of a large houre. In end, the King takes upe and dismisses him favourablie.

JOHN DURIE

The last night of Februar thairefter,[4] my father-in-law, Jhone Durie, departed this lyff; wha, as he leived happelie, walking with God in prayer day and night, sa he died, glorifeing God with grait joy and assurance of everlasting lyff and weillfear. For, efter he haid called for the Magistrats and Counsall of the brouche,[5] and exhorted tham, and admonished of certean things for thair weill, bathe togidder and severalie,[6] and siclyk [7] the Eldars of his Sessioun, and divers of the Breithring

---

[1] in a conciliatory way.   [2] beginning to touch on the matters at issue.
[3] argued.   [4] 1600. For John Durie see note on p. 43.
[5] burgh (i.e. Montrose).   [6] separately.   [7] in the same manner.

of the Ministerie ; and at last, efter he haid put his hous in ordour, and directed, instructed, and conforted his wyff and childring present, he takes him to privat meditatioun and prayer ; and thairefter inquyres what day of the monethe it was ; and being answerit to him, that it was the last of Februar, [and the morn the first of Merche,] " O ! then," sayes he, " the last day of my wretched pilgrimage, and the morn the first of my rest and glorie ! " Nocht lang thairefter, delyvering his saull in the hands of God, throw Jesus Chryst, leaning his head to his eldest sonnes breist, wha held him in his armes, maist quyetlie and sweitlie giffes upe the ghast. He was upright, zealus, and falon [1] familiar with God. Sa that, gif anie thing haid bein heavie and doutsome,[2] he haid na resolutioun, rest, nor releiff, till he haid fund it in meditatioun apart with God. And surlie, bathe in his particular turnes [3] and publict effeares, when things seimed falon hard, and dangerus, whowbeit of nature melancolius and feirfull,[4] he wald gett grait assurances ; as, namlie, of our retourn out of Eingland, and of our saiftie fra the Spainyars, he schew me oft tymes that his God assured him night and day thairof. Whatever haid com confortable to him, incontinent apart to prayer and thanksgiffing ; his haill conference and speaking upon the warks of God to the glorie of his name ; all uther things was (as he usit that word oft, " Tyntyme ") bot vanitie and tinsall of tyme [5] to him. Sa that I may say, the haill course of his lyff that I knew was an unweireing and constant occupatioun in doctrine, prayer, and praise. The mair I think on him, the mair I thank God that ever I knew him ; praying God, that, as I have sein the outgeat [6] of his conversatioun, (as the Apostle sayes, Heb. xiii. 7,) sa I may follow the sam in fathe. He oft regrated and inveyit upon the warldle fasones and bissines of the ministerie, saying, he fearit they sould becom als vyll in the peiple's eis as

---

[1] very.   [2] uncertain.   [3] in his own particular work.
[4] timid.   [5] loss of time. [6] utterance (literally " way out ").

ever the preists war. And as concerning this mater of
Bischopes, my uncle, Mr Andro, expressit his mynd
thairin in his Epitaphes, quhilk being maist pertinent
for that quhilk was, even at his deathe, in hand, I have
heir insert.[1] He desyrit, indeid, ernestlie to have levit
till the Assemblie, quhilk was hard at hand, that he
might have dischargit his mynd to the King and Breithring ; bot that quhilk alyve he could nocht, Mr Andro
supplied fathfullie efter his deathe. [It is guid to be
honest and upright in a guid cause ; for the guid cause
will honour sic a persone, bathe in lyff and deathe.]

MR ANDREW OFFERS HIS HEAD

My uncle, Mr Andro, cam to that Assemblie,[2] but
the King called for him and quarrelit him for his coming ;
wha, efter the auld maner, dischargit his conscience to
him with all fredome and zeall ; and, going from the
King in grait fervencie, said, putting his hand to his
crag [3] :—" Sir, tak yow this head, and gar [4] cut it af,
gif yie will ; yie sall sooner get it, or [5] I betray the cause
of Chryst ! " And sa he remeanit in the town all the
whyll, and furnisit arguments to the Breithring, and
mightelie strynthned and incuragit tham.

" FROM THE BED OF MY INFIRMITIE "

In the tyme of my seiknes,[6] the Generall Assemblie,
apointed to be hauldin in St Androis, was, be the King's
proclamation at Mercat-crosses, commandit to be keipit
with him at Brinteyland in the monethe of May. To
the quhilk, whowbeit seik and unable, it behoved me to
wryt. The quhilk Letter the King tuk out of the
Moderator's hand, and sufferit it nocht to be read, but
keipit it in his awin poutche,[7] and hes it leyed upe, as I
am informed, amangs his privie wryttes as yit ; for what

---

[1] The seven Latin epitaphs written by Andrew Melville have been
omitted.

[2] At Montrose, in March 1600.   [3] neck.

[4] cause.   [5] than.

[6] Melville had a serious illness in the spring of 1601.   [7] pocket.

purpose tyme will declar.   The copie wharof, word be
word, I thought thairfor guid to sett down heir :

   " *To the Godlie Fathers and Breithring convenit in this*
present Generall Assemblie at Brintyland, May 1601, J[ames]
M[elvill] wissethe grace, mercie, and peace from God throw Jesus
Chryst, with the spreit of fredome, uprightnes, and fathfulnes.

   " Havinge manie wayes a calling to be present with
yow at this Assemblie, (godlie Fathers and deir Breithring,) and steyit onlie be infirmitie of body, efter a
lang and soar seiknes, I could nocht at least bot
communicat my mynd with yow schortlie in wryt.   And
first, as concerning his Majestie : Sen it hes pleasit God
to indew him with sic a rare and singular grace, as to
resolve to bestow him selff, his stat, and all that God
hes giffen him in possessioun, or tytle, for glorefeing of
Chryst, King of Kings, in the meantenance of his Gospell
and trew Religioun ; and now to put hand to justice
against impietie, wrang, and all oppressioun, to kythe [1]
in effect the trew and ernest dispositioun of his hart.[2]
I think it all our partes to praise God uncessantlie thairfor,
and to concur and joyne with his Majestie in our calling
to our uttermaist, namlie in steiring upe and moving
the harts of his peiple to his reverence and obedience,
yea, to bestow thair lives and all that they have with his
Hines in that cause, and in all his Majestie's effeares
that may serve for the weill thairof.   And trewlie they
are worthie to be accursed, and nocht bruik the nam of
Christian nor Scottes men, bot esteimed enemies to God,
Relligioun, and his Hines, that will nocht willinglie
yield heirunto, as Deborah cryes, ' Curse Meros ! sayeth
the angell of the Lord, Curse ! because they cam nocht
to assist the Lord against the mightie.'   I wald wis,

   [1] Show.
   [2] To explain this, Melville added a note in the margin of his MS. :
" The King haid maid grait profession and promises anent Relligioun,
understanding that the Jesuittes in England war his conjurit enemies ;
and haid latlie execut justice upon grait personages for oppressioun
notablie."

thairfor, for this effect, as in the dayes of Asa and Joas, kings of Juda, namlie according to the derectioun of guid Jehoiada the priest, that solemne Covenants and Bands, the Word of God and prayer going befor, war maid betwix God and the King, God and the peiple, and betwix the King and the peiple, beginning in this present Assemblie, and sa going to Provincialles, Presbyteries, and throw everie Congregatioun of this land.

"Nixt, as concerning the Ministerie of Edinbruche, I hald fast that aggreiment of the Breithring conveinet in Brintyland in the monethe of Merche last [1]; and wald beseik the Breithring of the Assemblie till [2] insist with his Majestie, with the reasonnes set down at that Conference, and sic uther as God will furneise, joyning prayer to God, wha hes the King's hart in his hand, wherby his Hines might be brought to yeild thairunto, as a speciall weill, nocht onlie of the Kirk, but of his Majestie's esteat and effeares, (gif God hes giffen me anie eis to sie anie thing in tham.) For by [3] that, that the cheiff blokhous [4] of the Lord's Jerusalem in this land can nocht, in my judgment, be weill fortefied without tham. In my conscience, I knaw nocht braver trompettes to incurage, move, and sett fordwart the peiple to his Majestie's obedience and assistance, when occasioun of his Majestie's wechtiest effears may crave the sam. And trewlie, when I pas throw the formes of proceidings with my selff to spy out what may befall in end, I can nocht sie giff it be weill, bot it wilbe repossessioun [5]; for processes wilbe fund hard; transportatioun full of fascherie [6] and inconvenients, and in end fectles,[7] wanting contentment; thairfor the best mon be repossessioun, wherunto I pray God his Majestie's hart may be inclyned, as the haill Breitheringes ar, I am sure.

[1] The King had ordered the ministers of Edinburgh to leave the town and not to return. A number of ministers held a conference at Burntisland in March 1601, and resolved to petition the King.
[2] to.   [3] beyond.   [4] strong point.
[5] except it be repossession (*i.e.* restoration of the Edinburgh ministers to their charges).   [6] bother.   [7] spiritless, unenthusiastic.

" Bot ther is heir an incident (deir Breither) of graitter importance nor all the rest, wheranent I mon nocht onlie exhort you, bot, in the nam of Chryst, charge and adjure yow, as yie will answer to Him upon your fidelitie in his service, that yie endevour to redres it : This is, that interest quhilk Chryst sustenit be that act and decreit of Counsall, wherby the Ministers of Edinbruche ar deposit from pretching in anie tyme heirefter, because they refusit to pretche and giff thankes as was enjoyned to tham be the said Counsall [1] ; the graittest interest that ever Chryst sustenit in this land, for gif he hes nocht soll powar to chuse, call, and depose his awin messingers and ambassadours, he hes na powar at all. His Majestie hes schawin him selff, in my heiring divers tymes, willing that this sould be amendit ; bot I feir the decreit stands in the buiks without anie not thairupon. Forgett nocht this, bot remember it as the graittest poinct yie have to do. And let nocht, I humblie beseik, his Majestie and Counsall be miscontent with the bringing of this in heid, for the honour of Chryst, and feir of his just wrathe against sic as say, *Nolumus hunc regnare supra nos*, (Luc. xix. 14, 27,) constranes me ; the quhilk I wis to be als far from his Hienes and honourable Counsall, as from my awin hart and saull ; bot contrarie wayes, that in the favour, and be the blessing of Chryst, his throne, as the throne of David, may be established and florishe as the palme.

" Now, as to the rest, revise your Caveattes, for corruptioun creipes fast on, and is corroborat be custom ; sight [2] the conclusioun of your last Assemblie, and sie giff maters hes proceidit conform thairunto or nocht, giff it may pleise his Majestie to permit thir thinges to be done at this tyme, (quhilk indeid ar maist necessar to be done, utherwayes it is nocht possible to keipe fra corruptioun.) Fordar, the restraining of the fridome of

---

[1] They were willing to give thanks for the King's escape at the time of the Gowrie Conspiracy but refused to read from their pulpits his version of the affair.   [2] examine.

our Generall Assemblies in the ordinar Conventionnes thairof, wald be heavelie compleanit upon and regratit to his Majestie ; for, seing we have full powar and expres charge of Chryst, the onlie King of his Kirk, to meit and convein togidder for the government thairof, and hes our ordinarie Conventiones annes [1] in the yeir at least, and ofter *pro re nata*, approven be his Majestie in his lawes and actes of Parliament (Parl. 1592, Act 1,) [2] wharfor sould our meittings depend on licences, letters, and proclamationes, namlie whill uther esteattes, as of Barrones and Brouches, ar permitted to use ther privilage frelie ? Sall the Kirk of Jesus Chryst be les regardit, and restranit in hir fredome and privilage, in a setlit and constitut esteat, under the protectioun of a rare Christian Magistrat ? God forbid !

Finalie, my deir Breithring, charitie and the love of Chryst comands me to mak yow warning be my experience, that in all your speitches yie respect the trew profit of the Kirk, and of his Majestie's esteat joynit thairwith, and nocht present pleasuring. Now, the trew profit is that quhilk hes the warrand in the Law and the Prophetes, whowsoever the reasone of men think of it. We sould be the mouthe of God to all. His law sould be in our lippes, and trew wisdome in our mouthes. Our speitches sould be the speitches and oracles of God. And, as the lawers sayes, It is scham to speak without a law ; mikle mair, say we, It is scham befor God and his angeles, and befor the Kirk of God, to the dispensator of the heavinlie mysteries, to speak without Scriptoure and warrand of the Word of God. Tak head to this, utherwayes, when God beginnes to tak yow asyde and racken with yow, and ley on his hand, as I thank his fatherlie affectioun he hes done with me, yie will detest from your hart the facionnes of

[1] once.
[2] This is a reference to the " Golden Act "—" Ratification of the liberty of the trew Kirk : of Generall and Synodal assemblie : Of Presbyteries ; Of discipline. All Lawes of Idolatrie ar abrogate : Of presentation to benefices."

this warld ; the wisdome of fleche and bluid, the exemple
and maner of doing of this tyme in speciall ; yea, yie will
repent and rew [1] that ever yie knew or followed tham.

" In conclusioun, I ley down at your feit my Com-
missioun, as the pynnour [2] does his burding when he is
owerleyed.[3] It hes spendit that wharon my numerous
familie sould have bein susteined ; it hes greivit my
mynd continualie, and now, in end, it hes brought me
in extream danger of my lyff ; wharfor I beseik you
burding me na mair with it, unless yie wald have my
skine. Now, the Lord Jesus, of the sam love that moved
him to giff his lyff for his Kirk, govern and keipe the
sam fra the pollutionnes of this last age ; and mak us,
and all the laborars within the sam, ever myndfull of
that grait day when he sall com and call us to a compt
of our dispensatioun. Amen. From the bed of my
infirmitie, the 12 of May, 1601."

Whowbeit, the King conceallit this Letter, and wald
nocht suffer it to be red, yit he followit the advys of the
first part thairof, and renewit the Covenant,[4] to the
grait confort of all the Kirk at that Assemblie, and
ordeanit the sam to be done throwout the land. The
King ther, as I hard, maid a confortable confessioun of
his sinnes and his fathe ; and promesit, maist weghtelie
and solemnlie, to abhor all Papistrie, Idolatrie, and
Superstitioun, and to live and die in the trew Relligioun
wherin he was brought upe, and whilk was pretched
and professit within his realme of Scotland presentlie ;
also to execute justice, and do all dewties of a godlie and
Christian King, better than ever befor.

[1] rue.   [2] mason's labourer.   [3] over-burdened.
[4] In 1581 there was great alarm over Romanist tendencies at Court
and various insidious attempts to undermine the Kirk and re-establish
Roman Catholicism.   John Craig drew up a Covenant (usually called
the King's Confession or the Negative Confession) violently repudiating
the pope and all he stood for. The King subscribed it. This was the
Covenant to which he again swore in 1601. Craig (c. 1512-1600) was
Knox's colleague in Edinburgh from 1562 to 1571, and chaplain to
James VI from 1579 to 1594.